POET, PAINTER, AND PARSON:

The Life of John Dyer

Poet, Painter, and Parson:

The Life of John Dyer

By RALPH M. WILLIAMS

Assistant Professor of English
Trinity College

BOOKMAN ASSOCIATES

New York

To the Memory of
My Mother,
who shared with me the fun
of tracking down old documents.

JOHN DYER (1699-1757)

Artist unknown. Family tradition says that it was painted in Rome during
Dyer's visit there, 1724-25 (see p. 58). I am indebted to Ronald Hylton Smith,
Esq. of Cottingham, Yorkshire, for permission to reproduce here this portrait
and three paintings by Dyer himself.

Foreword

The two hundredth anniversary of the death of John Dyer is only a little over a year away as this book is going through the press. During these two centuries much has been printed in one place or another about the life of this versatile man, but never has it been adequately brought together into a proper biography. This lack I am attempting to remedy in this volume, supplementing the printed sources with material from family papers and other manuscript sources. These have enabled me to present here a more complete outline of Dyer's life than has been heretofore available, although the destructiveness of time will be only too evident in some of the details which I have not been able to fill in.

The most tantalizing loss, because we know so much about what has been lost, and the loss has occurred so recently, has been the scattering of Dyer's own papers. They were, apparently, kept intact for four generations, descending through Dyer's daughter Elizabeth to her great-grandson, William Hylton Dyer Longstaffe. Trained as a lawyer, but better known as an antiquary, Longstaffe printed some material from Dyer's papers, but his interest generally tended to be genealogical rather than literary. He provided the material for Willmott's biography and edition of the poems, a fact which in part explains the inadequacy of both, although they have been indispensable to the student of Dyer for over a hundred years.

At Longstaffe's death in 1898, and again after the death of his son, James Ensor Dyer Longstaffe, in 1902, sales were held, and at one or both of them many of the Dyer papers were sold, leaving comparatively little as was discovered by Mr. Alfred H. Collins when writing his essay for the Master of Arts degree at London University in 1930. But even since then—perhaps after the death of Longstaffe's daughter, Mrs. Ronald Smith, in 1934 —there have been losses; in 1937 when I first visited Mrs. Smith's son, the present representative of the family, Dyer's sermons, which Collins had seen, had disappeared.

Other branches of the family owned Dyeriana also. Whatever manuscripts Thomas Dyer, the poet's younger brother, may have had, did not come down as a unit. John's letters to his brother descended in one line and were destroyed in the 1920's by a descendant who felt that no one today would be interested in John Dyer. Some manuscripts of poetry (possibly those willed to him for publication by John?) went to Thomas's eldest son, and also disappeared, though not by destruction I hope, about 1920. At Aberglasney, at a sale in 1914, Dyer's manuscript of a book of *The Fleece* was sold, and perhaps other material.

Except for a number of paintings in various media, and a few memorabilia such as a Bible, the carved ivory head of his walking stick, and his seal, all that remains in the possession of the family are a handful of notebooks. These have been taken apart by Longstaffe (if, indeed, they had not fallen apart before) and the single leaves (occasionally double, conjugate leaves) have been mounted on the stubs of leaves of a much larger book. Longstaffe disarranged the order of some of them slightly, but as the size of the original leaves varies from notebook to notebook, it is possible to identify at least seven different notebooks of different sizes. Lettering them arbitrarily as they first appear, we find:

A. Not really a notebook, but two leaves of quarto-size paper, with Dyer's summary of pages 2 and 9 of the anonymous 1745 translation of Columella's *De Re Rustica*.

B. The "Mapleton Notebook," our chief source of information regarding Dyer from 1734 to 1737.

C. A book used from 1728 or 1729 to the end of his life for fair copies of his shorter poems. Characteristically, it contains a sketch of a brooder for his henhouse.

D. The earliest of these notebooks, probably having been pretty well completed during 1722-23, with a few additions made around 1737.

E. The "Worcester Notebook," one of the main sources of information about Dyer's movements from 1736-40.

F. Another Worcester notebook, mainly a commonplace book, but with the extracts from reading much interrupted by business notes and other extraneous matter.

G. Another, more serious, commonplace book, the first part for prose, the second for poetry, both begun in 1737.

H. Another, still more serious, commonplace book, kept from 1736 to 1741, resumed in 1750, and containing Prayers and Meditations dated 1727, apparently copied from an earlier notebook now lost. This book contains much soul-searching on Dyer's part.

Longstaffe called the finished volume, rather inaccurately, "Miscellaneous Transactions, 1726-1740." The title does, however, suggest that he may have treated all Dyer's notebooks in this way, attempting some sort of classification or unified subject matter in each new volume, and that these notebooks defied inclusion elsewhere. Longstaffe's collections pertaining to the history of the county of Durham were sold to the Dean and Chapter of the Cathedral at Durham. Accidentally mixed in was a similar collection of Dyer material—Dyer's fair copy of "A Plan of a Commercial Map of England" and the notebooks which he made in preparing it. Presumably other similarly unified groups of Dyer's notebooks once existed also.

Except for C and a few scraps of verse scattered through the others, there is little poetry in these notebooks. It is here that the loss seems most grievous. I have, consequently, not attempted too much in the way of literary criticism in this volume, for it is difficult, if not impossible, to evaluate Dyer's work when one does not know what his final wishes were for his works as he left them for his brother Thomas to publish. I am, rather, hoping that this book will come into the right hands to bring to light enough of the missing manuscripts to enable me to make a more definitive estimate of his work at another time.

II

We might pause for a moment to consider the attitude of Thomas Dyer's descendant who felt that no one would be interested in John Dyer in the twentieth century. Obviously I do not agree with her, as I have written a book about him. Why, then, should anyone read about Dyer?

I hope I need not justify here the study of history. For me part of the fascination of the eighteenth century lies in the fact that we know enough about it and its people to feel intimately acquainted, and we find it a period very much like our own. For example, Dyer in his shifting from one profession to another, from lawyer to painter to farmer to clergyman (poetry, I am afraid, was usually secondary for him), is very similar to many young men today who try first one thing and then another. We may blame this phenomenon today on the after-effects of the late war, or the upsetting circumstance of the draft and compulsory military service, but actually I think its cause lies much deeper. This sort of restlessness is characteristic of sensitive young people in a period of transition. The change may be different in each period, but it is there in both. Today we are wavering between hopeful idealism and discouraged cynicism, between faith in and fear of science and reason. The eighteenth century, when it began, had high hopes for Reason and Newtonian science; it was the Age of Reason and Enlightenment. But Reason and Science proved wanting, and in Dyer we see in miniature the entire eighteenth century's stumbling progression towards Romanticism, sometimes even turning back upon itself. It is from this point of view that I have tried to unify all the various facets of Dyer's career.

Dyer, although an excellent character from which to view a century, is, of course, more than just a representative of his times. His life has an intrinsic merit also, as we watch him meeting illness, defeat, and discouragement, and rising above them. This character, as Johnson says in the sixtieth *Rambler*, it is the business of the biographer to make clear, insofar as the materials left to him make it possible.

And finally, we must not forget, in spite of what I have said before, that it is primarily as a man of letters that Dyer has been remembered. Later in the eighteenth century he was considered important enough to be included by Johnson in *The Lives of the Poets,* and *Grongar Hill* has been able to hold its own with modern readers of poetry on its own merits, not just because of its historical significance. I have tried to show in this volume how closely Dyer's life was related to his poetry, and how it influenced what he wrote.

III

This work began as a collaboration. Dr. Edward A. Parker had written a thesis on Dyer at Oxford; I had written a doctor's dissertation on Dyer at Yale. In August, 1939, we agreed that we could produce a better book by collaborating than by competing, and so entered upon a plan which only a world war and other distractions have kept Dr. Parker from completing his share in. It has seemed best, at this point, to go ahead with the publication of my share—the biography—and hope that Dr. Parker will soon find time to finish his work on Dyer's reading and Dyer as an economist. Although his contribution to this volume is not as great as we had once hoped it would be, it is not inconsiderable. Dr. Parker undertook the drudgery of measuring the size of each page and sorting out the remaining notebooks by Dyer, a bit of detective work fundamental to our study and beautifully executed by him. In addition, Dr. Parker has read and commented upon all eight of my chapters, some of them in more than one version, and over a period of so many years that I cannot now recall all the points at which he has improved my work. At one or two places I have been able to acknowledge my indebtedness in footnotes; for the rest, I hope he will accept this note as my sincere, though inadequate, thanks for all his help.

To the distinguished teacher and scholar who first interested me in John Dyer I wish to express my gratitude. Professor Chauncey B. Tinker, who directed my dissertation on Dyer and whose famous seminar in the Age of Johnson first inspired me and many others with a love for the period to which he has given so much light, it is impossible for me to thank adequately. The great resources of his library, his mind, his heart, have all been at the service of his students; I hope he will find the following pages worthy of his loyalty.

This book could not, of course, have been written by anyone without the very courteous and generous cooperation which I have received from the present representative of the Dyer family, Ronald Hylton Smith, Esq., of Cottingham, Yorkshire. His family papers, portraits, and other relics of interest have been completely at my service, and in addition to adding much new information about Dyer, have helped to clarify a great deal of what Longstaffe had printed in the last century.

I wish also to express my gratitude to the owners of two other private libraries which have been of great help to me. His Grace, the late Duke of Northumberland, very kindly allowed me to use the library at Alnwick Castle in the summer of 1936. Here the papers of the Countess of Hertford yielded a rich harvest, as the following pages will show. And Mr. W. S. Lewis, of Farmington, Connecticut, has, with his customary generosity, allowed me access to the treasures of his library. Although best known as a collector and editor of Horace Walpole, Mr. Lewis has a collection of such breadth that it is of use to every eighteenth-century scholar.

I have, in the course of twenty years, written to or called upon many persons—too many to mention here individually—in search of letters, notebooks, sketchbooks, paintings, records of Dyer of every sort. Almost invariably my reception has been cordial, and I should like to acknowledge more fully all the kindnesses which I have received, especially from the clergy of the Church of England, many of whom I have bothered in hunting for entries in church registers concerning Dyer and his family. A few I have acknowledged in my footnotes, but many on whom I imposed in vain must go unmentioned here—though not unthanked in spirit.

Among public institutions I am, naturally, most indebted to the three great repositories of eighteenth-century material, the

British Museum, the Bodleian Library, and the Sterling Memorial Library at Yale University. To the staffs of these libraries I am sincerely obliged for their patience and help. The diocesan record offices established by most of the dioceses in England have been very helpful also; to the staffs of those in Lincoln, Worcester, and Hereford I am especially grateful. I am also much indebted to the Dean and Chapter of the Cathedral at Durham for permission to photograph and use the manuscript of Dyer's "Commercial Map" and its notebooks. And in the mazes of the Public Record Office and Somerset House most scholars need guidance; to the staffs of both these repositories I owe much for their unfailing patience and helpfulness.

I wish also to express my appreciation to the Dean and Faculty of the Graduate School of Yale University for accepting a fairly regular production of articles on Dyer as evidence of good faith on my part that I ultimately expected to publish my dissertation in book form. This is a considerably revised version of my dissertation, but it has been, I think, improved by the revision. I appreciate their acceptance of this volume as fulfillment of the requirement that a major portion of the doctoral dissertation be published.

R. M. W.

Trinity College
Hartford, Connecticut

Table of Contents

Table of Illustrations

List of Cue Titles Used

The following works represent the most frequently referred to, though not necessarily the most important, sources of information concerning John Dyer's life; a more nearly complete bibliography may be compiled by consulting the footnotes. In quoting from both printed and manuscript sources I have modernized the spelling, punctuation, and capitalization and expanded all contractions and abbreviations. In quoting from Dyer's notebooks passages which he had taken from printed sources, I have quoted the passage as Dyer wrote it and given a page reference to an edition of the work which I think he may have used (or which fits his page reference if he gives one). As Dyer quotes, condenses, and paraphrases at will, his version sometimes is a very inexact quotation from the passage to which I give a reference.

Cue Titles	*Full References*
Add. Ms.	Additional Manuscript, in the British Museum, London. In particular:
	Add. Ms. 35,401. The Hardwicke Papers: Letters of Daniel Wray to Philip Yorke (Viscount Royston from 1754), 1740-67.
	Add. Ms. 29,300, fol. 119. Dyer's letter to Duncombe, Jan. 31, 1757.
Alnwick Ms.	Alnwick Manuscript, in the library of His Grace the Duke of Northumberland at Alnwick Castle. In particular:
	Alnwick Ms. 22. Percy Family Letters and Papers.
	Alnwick Ms. 115. "Meditations and Prayers for the Time of Sickness. Written in the Year 1728." By the Countess of Hertford.

Cue Titles	*Full References*
	Alnwick Ms. 116. "A Miscellany of Verse and Prose. Begun March the 5th, 1725/26." By the Countess of Hertford.
CHEL	*Cambridge History of English Literature,* ed. A. W. Ward and A. R. Waller, 15 vols. (Cambridge, Cambridge Univ. Press, 1907-16).
Collations and Additions	*Collations and Additions to the Poems of John Dyer, L.L.B.,* by William Hylton Dyer Longstaffe. I refer to it only for material not printed in Willmott (q.v.) or *The Patrician* (q.v.).
DNB	*The Dictionary of National Biography,* edited by Sir Leslie Stephen. 63 vols. (London, 1885-1900).
Duncombe's *Letters*	Duncombe, John (ed.): *Letters by Several Eminent Persons Deceased.* 3 vols. (London, 1773). One of Dyer's letters is also reprinted in the review of this collection in the *Monthly Review,* XLVIII (1773), 35-6.
GM	*The Gentleman's Magazine* (London, 1731-1907).
Green	Green, Francis: "The Dyers of Aberglasney," *Transactions of the Historical Society of West Wales,* VII (1917-8), 93-108.
Johnson's *Lives*	Johnson, Samuel: *The Lives of the English Poets,* edited by George B. Hill, 3 vols. (Oxford, 1905).

Cue Titles	Full References
L.A.O.	Lincolnshire Archives Office, Exchequer Gate, Lincoln, where the Lincoln Diocesan Records are deposited. The particular work and volume number follow this abbreviation.
Lewis' *Miscellany*	Lewis, David (ed.): *Miscellaneous Poems by Several Hands*, 2 vols. (London, 1726-30).
Montgomeryshire Collections	Longstaffe, William Hylton Dyer: "John Dyer as a Painter," *Collections Historical and Archaeological relating to Montgomeryshire* (usually known as *Montgomeryshire Collections*), XI (1878), 396-402.
Mod. Phil.	*Modern Philology* (Chicago, 1903+). In particular: Hughes, Helen Sard: "John Dyer and the Countess of Hertford," XXVII (1929-30), 311-20.
Ms. Bodl.	Manuscript Bodleian, in the Bodleian Library, Oxford. In particular: Mss. Bodl. 1007-1012: The books into which Thomas Edwards copied many of his letters.
Nichols' *Illustrations*	Nichols, John: *Illustrations of the Literary History of the Eighteenth Century*, 8 vols. (London, 1817-58).
Nichols' *LA*	Nichols, John: *Literary Anecdotes of the Eighteenth Century*, 9 vols. (London, 1812-15).
N&Q	*Notes and Queries:* A Medium of Inter-Communication for Literary Men . . . etc. (London, 1849+).

Cue Titles	*Full References*
P.R.O.	Public Record Office, in Chancery Lane, London. Chancery Proceedings are indicated by the initial letter *C* in the shelf-mark, the King's Bench by *K.B.*, and the State Papers by *S.P.*
Savage's *Miscellany*	Savage, Richard (ed.): *Miscellaneous Poems and Translations. By Several Hands.* (London, 1726).
TCAS	*Transactions of the Carmarthenshire Antiquarian Society* (Carmarthen, 1905-39). Succeeded by *The Carmarthen Antiquary.*
The Patrician	*The Patrician*, ed. J. B. Burke. 6 vols. (all published; London, 1846-8). In particular the articles by William Hylton Dyer Longstaffe, "Notes respecting the Life and Family of John Dyer, the Poet," IV (1847), 7-12, 264-8, 420-6; V (1848), 75-81, 218-35.
Victor, *Original Letters*	Victor, Benjamin: *Original Letters, Dramatic Pieces, and Poems,* 3 vols. (London, 1776).
Willmott	Willmott, Robert Aris (ed.): *The Poetical Works of Mark Akenside and John Dyer* (London, 1855).

CHAPTER I

"Within the Groves of Grongar Hill"

The earliest record we have of John Dyer, the man who later made himself famous as the author of *Grongar Hill* and *The Fleece,* is the entry of his baptism on the 13th of August, 1699, in the parish register of Llanfynnydd, Carmarthenshire. He was the fourth child of Robert and Catherine Cocks Dyer, and judging from the regularity with which they had their children baptized,[1] one would believe that they followed the usual practice of baptizing a child within a fortnight of its birth.

Llanfynnydd today is a quiet little village, beautifully situated among the hills about four miles north of the main road from Carmarthen to Llandilo, and about five miles from Grongar Hill. As you drive north to Llanfynnydd past Court Henry, you pass over several ridges of hills, from the top of each of which the valley below, with its fields separated from one another by hedges, looks like the inverted vaulting of some great cathedral. The country is primarily agricultural, and has probably changed very little since John Dyer spent his boyhood here.

John seems to have lived a normal childhood. The Dyers' residence,[2] like most country dwellings of the time, was fairly

---

[1] I am indebted to the Rev. D. J. Davies, Vicar of Llanfynnydd, for showing me the following entries concerning the Dyer family in the register of his church:

Elizabeth, bapt. Jan. 25, 1695/6; buried Jan. 26, 1695/6
John, bapt. Feb. 2, 1696/7; buried Mar. 20, 1697/8
Robert, bapt. Mar. 17, 1697/8
John, bapt. Aug. 13, 1699 [the poet]
Thomas, bapt. Oct. 28, 1700
Francesca, bapt. June 22, 1703; buried Sept. 16, 1703
Bennet, bapt. Aug. 22, 1704

[2] The legend is that the Dyers lived at Whitlera Farm in Llanfynnydd and kept a fulling mill and dyed cloth (*TCAS,* II [1906-7],

self-sufficient and provided them with most of their supplies: the garden and livestock with vegetables and meat, and such household industries as brewing beer and ale and making cheese, with other edibles. The usual mishaps to be expected from such an environment occurred, of course; some of the more spectacular ones he recorded later in life in a "Journal of Escapes"— possibly for the amusement of his children. In 1704, for example, he fell into a tub of scalding wort and had to be rescued, and later in the same year he fell on a case knife which, wanting a handle, was stuck upright in the ground and penetrated deep into his throat.[3]

Sometime after the baptism of their son Bennet in August, 1704, and before April, 1709, when Robert Dyer bought two farms in Llanvihangel Rhos Y Corn and was referred to in the

---

163, referring to an article in an issue of *The Welshman* for August, 1864, which I have been unable to see). This story, however, seems highly improbable. Mr. J. Davies, the present owner, very kindly looked up the deeds of the farm for me but found that they go back only to the nineteenth century and so are of no help. The present house was there in Robert Dyer's time, and seems much too small to have housed a rising young solicitor and family of four sons. It is in a solitary location, up a small valley by itself, between two and three miles from Llanfynnydd, too isolated a spot, it would seem, for an ambitious young man to choose for his home when much of his business was in Carmarthen. Tradition must, of course, be given its weight, especially when I can offer no substitute for Whitlera as the Dyers' residence; there may have been reasons for being out of the world, or there may have been a larger house on the farm then. The story that the Dyers kept a fulling mill for the dyeing of cloth sounds suspiciously like an invention suggested by the family name. There is no evidence that Robert Dyer ever followed any other profession than that of solicitor, and there is no stream in this valley large enough to drive a fuller's mill.

[3] *The Patrician,* IV (1847), 264; *Montgomeryshire Collections,* XI (1878), 397. The Ms. of the "Journal of Escapes" came ultimately into the hands of John Dyer's great-great-grandson, William Hylton Dyer Longstaffe, and was probably sold at one of the sales in 1898 or 1902. Its present location is not known.

deeds as "of Aberglasney," [4] the Dyers moved from Llanfynnydd to Aberglasney in the nearby parish of Llangathen, where they and their descendants lived, first as tenants, then as owners, for the rest of the century.[5] Several considerations influenced this change of residence. One was that increased financial prosperity enabled them to live in greater comfort; another was that their home in Llanfynnydd may have become too small for four growing boys; important also was the fact that Aberglasney had at one time belonged to ancestors of Robert Dyer's mother.

From the time of the Norman penetration into South Wales to the reign of Henry VIII, Aberglasney had been a monastic foundation. At the dissolution of the monasteries or shortly thereafter, the estate became the property of Sir William Thomas,[6] from whom Robert Dyer's mother (who was born Mary Williams of Brynhavod, an estate in Llangathen not far from Aberglasney) was descended.[7] About 1600 the Thomas family sold Aberglasney to the family of Anthony Rudd, Bishop of St. David's, who is thought to have done considerable building and altering on the estate.[8] The Rudds kept Aberglasney until very early in the eighteenth century when, at the insolvency of Sir Rice Rudd, Bart., all his property was sold by decree of the Court of Chancery to Sir Thomas Watson-Wentworth, of Wentworth Woodhouse, Yorkshire, who in turn sold all these

---

[4] National Library of Wales, Carmarthen Town Deeds Nos. 2 and 6.

[5] *TCAS,* II (1906-7), 157, 162; Green, pp. 101, 107-8.

[6] Sir William Thomas was living at Aberglasney when he was appointed sheriff of Carmarthenshire (for a second term) in 1540 (*TCAS,* II [1906-7], 157). He leased Carmarthen Priory from the crown on May 20, 1538, and doubtless in some similar manner acquired Aberglasney as a reward for his services as a witness for the king in the divorce trial of Henry VIII and Katherine of Aragon (*Letters and Papers, Foreign and Domestic, of the Reign of Henry VIII* [London, 1870-1898], IV, 873, 2578; XIII, part i, 584; XVI, 644).

[7] *The Patrician,* IV (1847), 7, 10.

[8] *TCAS,* II (1906-7), 157.

properties (including much more than Aberglasney) to Robert Dyer in June, 1710.

An amusing legend is recorded in the *Montgomeryshire Collections* of the unwillingness of the previous occupants to give up Aberglasney to the Dyers, who lived there for some years as tenants before purchasing it in 1710:

> Aberglasney is said to have been purchased by [John] Dyer's father, Robert, a successful solicitor, under a decree of the Court of Chancery, on the insolvency of Sir Rice Rudd after a severely contested election, and on terms so favorable to the purchaser that he resold detached farms for prices sufficient to pay for the whole estate. An old tenant who died aged 85, told the late owner, Mr. Walters Philipps,[9] that his grandfather had witnessed a bloody contest between the Rudd and Dyer parties about possession, Dyer bringing in a strong force of strangers and ultimately succeeding.[10]

Much of this story is true, in spite of the omission of Sir Thomas Watson-Wentworth as an intervening owner between Sir Rice Rudd, Bart., and Robert Dyer; the battle could have occurred when the Dyers sought to take possession as tenants of Sir Thomas. And the records of lawsuits arising out of the estate of Robert Dyer and the settling of his estate substantiate the first part of the story; they show that he acquired the extensive property of Sir Rice Rudd for £8601, including not only Aberglasney and the farms attached to it, but the Lordship and Priory of Kidwelly with the numerous farms belonging to it, and miscellaneous pieces of property as well in some ten parishes of Carmarthenshire. Of the total purchase price, Robert Dyer paid £2201 at the time of purchase; in 1715 he sold eight scattered farms in Llangunnor and Kidwelly for £3838/8/6, and was thus able to pay off £4000 of the principal and all the interest up to that date. The remaining principal (£2400) and inter-

---

[9] I.e., John Walters-Philipps, nephew of the Thomas Philipps who bought Aberglasney from the Dyers (*TCAS,* II [1906-7], 157; Green, p. 108).

[10] *Montgomeryshire Collections,* XI (1878), 396.

est which had accumulated in the meantime was finally paid by Robert Dyer, Jr. in 1727 by the sale of the Lordship and Priory of Kidwelly, so that ultimately Aberglasney, and considerable other property as well, cost the Dyer family only the down payment, a fact easily distorted by hearsay into what the story says.[11]

During these years John Dyer was attending school also. One of his early biographers reports that he received "the elementary part of his education in the country,"[12] but does not say specifically to what school, if any, he went, or whether he was privately tutored. The churchwardens' presentments for 1684 list small schools in both Llanfynnydd and Llangathen,[13] and if they were still in existence in the first decade of the eighteenth century, he may have attended one or both of them. Or he may have attended the famous Queen Elizabeth's Grammar School in Carmarthen, although there is no real evidence that he did so.[14]

John Dyer did, however, go to Westminster School. He is usually said to have been there under Dr. Freind, who was headmaster from 1711 to 1733. But as he is not mentioned in the extant records of admissions, which begin in 1714, and as one incident dated 1714 was most likely to occur in his first year, I believe that he came up to Westminster in the autumn of 1713. His older brother Robert may have been at the school also

---

[11] Lloyd vs. Dyer, P.R.O., C.11.995/14; C.11.1229/41 & 43; Dyer vs. Dyer, P.R.O., C.11.1260/6; C.33.349, foll. 504-5. For more details concerning the transactions leading up to Robert Dyer's purchase of Aberglasney, see my article, "The Dyer Family of Aberglasney," *The Carmarthen Antiquary,* number 1 (Carmarthen, 1941), 30-42.

[12] Thomas Rees, *The Beauties of England and Wales,* Vol. XVIII, *South Wales* (London, 1815), p. 326.

[13] *TCAS,* X (1914-5), 98-9.

[14] No record of admissions is extant before the year 1857 (*TCAS,* II [1906-7], 216). In his "Journal of Escapes," however, Dyer does mention falling into Job's Well in Carmarthen in 1709, suggesting that he at least went to Carmarthen without too close supervision at the age of ten—see *The Patrician,* IV (1847), 264.

during this year, before going on to Balliol College, Oxford, in 1714;[15] if John stayed that long (which is doubtful), he would later have had the company of his younger brothers, Thomas and Bennet, who came up in 1717.[16]

The school at this time numbered close to four hundred boys. Most of them lived in boarding houses nearby, each of which was presided over by an "usher," one of the undermasters who lived in the house and enforced discipline for the landlady.[17] The old dormitory during Dyer's stay at Westminster was in a very dilapidated state, and in spite of Dean Atterbury's efforts, the new one was not completed until about 1730, so the chances are that Dyer lived in one of the boarding houses.[18]

The curriculum emphasized the study of grammar. In the lowest, or "petty," form the boys began with the study of English grammar and Latin conjugations and declensions; by the end of the second form, the study of Latin grammar had completely replaced that of English grammar. Many of the subjects which we consider important today—geography, history, mathematics, for example—were learned through the Latin authors studied. Monday morning was reserved for a study of the catechism, or, in the lower and upper third forms, of Bishop Williams' *Explanation of the Catechism*. Tuesday afternoon was usually a holiday.[19]

---

[15] He was then rather curiously described as the son of R. Dyer of Llanvynny (Llanfynnydd)—see Green, p. 104.

[16] G. F. Russell Barker, *The Record of Old Westminsters* (London, 1928), I, 296; II, 1068; supplementary volume, ed. by J. B. Whitmore and G. R. V. Radcliffe (London, ca. 1938), pp. 50-51.

[17] John Sargeaunt, *Annals of Westminster School* (London, 1898), p. 158.

[18] J. D. Carleton, *Westminster*, "English Public Schools" Series (London, 1938), pp. 23-4.

[19] Letter of Thomas Barnett to Thomas Percy, Oct. 16, 1771, discussing the curriculum at Westminster about 1730, when Barnett was there. See *The Elizabethan*, XIX (Westminster School, 1930), 315-6.

Dyer has left us no record of his participation in extra-curricular activities. The annual play was the thing most likely to attract him. In a more or less regular rotation, four plays were given every four years, one each year: George Ruggle's famous farce, *Ignoramus,* and Terence's *Amphitryon, Eunuchus,* and *Phormio.* Dyer must have seen one or more of these plays during his stay at Westminster. Football of a primitive sort seems to have been the chief sport indulged in by the boys, and as a generation later another poet, William Cowper, boasted of his proficiency at the game, there is no reason for not supposing that John Dyer took part also.[20]

That John Dyer did not like Westminster, at least at first, is very clear. In his "Journal of Escapes" under the year 1714 he later wrote, "Ran from school and my father, on a box of the ear being given me. Strolled for three or four days—found at Windsor." [21] Just what part his father played in this episode is not clear, but as we shall see later, a bad lack of understanding existed between John and his father. In spite of these difficulties, however, Dyer did gain one thing from his stay at Westminster which he appreciated—the friendship of several persons whose tastes were much like his own. When he returned to London in the 1720's, he renewed these acquaintances, with the literary results which may be seen in David Lewis's *Miscellany.*[22] Among these friends were David Lewis and Samuel Wesley, who were ushers, and Vincent Bourne and Isaac Hawkins Browne, who were students, about the time that Dyer was at Westminster.

Just when Dyer left Westminster is not known. He may have stayed until 1716 or 1717, or his father, disgusted by his attitude in running away, may have brought him home in 1714. In any

---

[20] Sargeaunt, pp. 130-3.

[21] *The Patrician,* IV (1847), 264. It seems to me that such an event would be most likely to occur during a boy's first year at school; for this reason I believe that Dyer went up to Westminster in the autumn of 1713 and that this episode took place in the spring of 1714.

[22] D[avid] Lewis, ed., *Miscellaneous Poems, by Several Hands,* 2 vols. (London, 1726-30), I, 195-6, 223-31.

case, he seems not to have finished the usual course of studies at
the school, for in middle life he retained little of what he should
have learned at Westminster. In his notebooks later he quotes
many of the Latin authors whom he should have read at Westminster—and quotes from English translations. He even went
back to one of his school grammars to refresh his memory.[23]
Although he was able to translate for himself a few scraps from
Cicero and Columella, he never shows the familiarity with Latin
authors that his friends Thomas Edwards and Daniel Wray do
in their letters.

It is with his return to Aberglasney, to enter his father's office
to study law, that the true biography of John Dyer begins, for
it is here that we first begin to know something of his personality
and see for the first time the conflict in him between the dreamy
romantic and the practical man of business that runs through
all his life. Aberglasney and the country around it were certainly
well suited to develop the romantic in John, and his lifelong
interest in scenery and antiquities may be traced directly back
to this environment. Remains of the old monastic buildings can
still be seen at Aberglasney, and they may well have been more
extensive in his time. The old chapel has become the kitchen
and laundry of the new mansion; the coach-house wall, very
thick and loopholed for bows and arrows, was part of one of
the old buildings; and the walled terrace at the rear of the house
was supported by arches which were probably the cloister con-
necting the chapel and the main building. A fine towered gate-
way with Romanesque arch stands on the front lawn, and a well
preserved Norman arch forms the entrance into the stable yard.[24]

---

[23] *A Short Introduction to Grammar, for the Use of the Lower
Forms, in the King's School at Westminster.* Dyer mentions this
book in a list in notebook E. What edition he had is not known.

[24] Colonel Mayhew, "Aberglasney," *TCAS,* II (1906-7), 156-7.
Colonel Mayhew lived at Aberglasney early in the twentieth century. His article is quoted by The Royal Commission on Ancient
and Historical Monuments, *An Inventory of the Ancient Monuments in Wales and Monmouthshire,* Vol. V, *The County of Carmarthen* (London, 1917), p. 156.

It is not surprising that a boy with a mind as sensitive as John Dyer's, growing up in such surroundings, should develop an interest in antiquities.

This interest was further fostered, and connected with his love of nature, by Grongar Hill, at whose foot Aberglasney is situated. The Welsh name, "Y Gron Gaer," meaning "the circular fort," was taken from the ancient and sizable earthworks on the top of the hill. From them can be seen the ruins of four medieval castles[25] mentioned in Dyer's poem *Grongar Hill:*

> Old castles on the cliffs arise,
> Proudly towering in the skies!   (49-50)

The numerous fortifications in the vicinity well support a statement made by a modern writer on the area, that it was so beautiful that the inhabitants felt it well worth fighting for.[26] The valley of the Towy River, at the foot of Grongar Hill, is indeed attractive. The neat little farms appear much neater with their boundaries set off by the usual hedges; the wooded areas, such as that at Golden Grove, where Jeremy Taylor wrote his *Holy Living and Holy Dying,* provide a great variety of color. The quiet, peaceful valley contrasts with the rocky hills surrounding it, and the pleasant farms with the ruined towers. As Dyer said in *Grongar Hill,*

> Each give each a double charm,
> As pearls upon an AEthiop's arm.   (112-3)

Although Dyer enjoyed Aberglasney and its environs thoroughly, we must not think of him as spending all his leisure time "within the groves of Grongar Hill," (l. 158) in solitary dreaming under the blackthorn tree as he is portrayed in the frontispiece to the first collected edition of his poems (1761). At home he had the companionship of his three brothers during

---

[25] Castle Kilkenning, Castle Carreg, Dinevawr Castle, Dryslwyn Castle—Willmott, p. 4, who cites Dyer's Ms.

[26] Charles Harper, *The Oxford, Gloucester, and Milford Haven Road* (London, 1905), II, 215.

their vacations from school and of his father's apprentice, Howell
Williams, who lived with the Dyers during his apprenticeship and
carried on the business of Robert Dyer, Sr. for the family until
1725.[27] In *Grongar Hill* he mentions the "Haunt of Phyllis,
queen of love" (l. 64) as being visible from the top of the hill,
and among his unpublished poems are three "On the Death of
Phyllis." And he must have had many other friends in this neighborhood, although we now know nothing of them.

Neither should we think that, because Dyer later gave up
the law as a profession, he merely dabbled at the subject and
took every occasion to avoid work. The lawsuits in which he
was later involved give evidence that he learned the business of
a solicitor quite well in the years that he was working at it. And
still later he used his knowledge of the law to good advantage
in managing his own property and was the only one of the four
sons of Robert Dyer, Sr. to keep his business affairs consistently
in good order.

Robert Dyer, Sr. undoubtedly saw this ability in John and
for this reason brought him back to help out in his own office
instead of sending him to one of the inns of court or chancery.
The father apparently tried to develop the boy's talents for practical matters at the expense of his artistic inclinations; family
tradition reports that Robert Dyer the elder frowned heavily
upon all of John's endeavors at painting or poetry,[28] and this
story is given indirect support by the inventory of the elder Dyer's
estate. At the time of his death Robert Dyer, Sr. owned only
two pictures, each a family portrait probably acquired for
genealogical rather than artistic reasons. And his books, valued
at only five pounds, probably consisted mainly of law volumes.[29]

---

[27] Woodroffe vs. Seys, P.R.O., C.11.1021/30. In his deposition
Howell Williams says that he was "articled or lettered clerk to and
with the said Robert Dyer" in January, 1713/4, when he was 17
years old, that he lived with the Dyer family until 1721, and conducted much of the elder Dyer's business for the family until 1725.

[28] *Montgomeryshire Collections,* XI (1878), 397.

[29] Woodroffe vs. Dyer, P.R.O., C.11.1022/27. For further details concerning the inventory and the character of Robert Dyer,

Fortunately the boy who was independent enough in 1714 to run away from Westminster and his father did not let that father crush his taste for the arts. The law appealed to the practical side of Dyer's nature, but at this point in his life his chief interest was in painting and poetry, especially painting. Perhaps fortunately for Dyer, all his early paintings are now either unidentifiable or lost, and only one or two of his youthful effusions in verse remain.[30] One of these, which Longstaffe thought was an early version of *Grongar Hill,* was printed by Willmott in his introduction to the later poem.[31] Of all his various activities, his study of the law seems to have had the least effect upon his

---

see my article, "Robert Dyer the elder of Aberglasney, Gent.," *The Carmarthen Antiquary,* II, part iii (1951 for 1947-8), 75-88.

[30] At Aberglasney today is a copy of *A New Version of the Psalms of David,* by N. Brady and N. Tate (London, 1718) with the signature (twice) of Jonathan Dyer on the verso of the title page, in a hand very much like that of John Dyer a few years later. Between the signatures are the following verses, dated 1718:

> Death comes for, as you see,
> Both rich and poor,
> To old and young;
> He doth not miss a door
> To which he's sent
> To fetch them hence away.
> Their glass being run,
> They must no longer stay.

(The punctuation is mine, there being none in the original; I have modernized the capitalization also.) I know of no Jonathan Dyer connected with the Aberglasney Dyers. If then this is John Dyer expanding his name to Jonathan, these verses may be added to the so-called early version of *Grongar Hill* as a second piece of Dyer's juvenilia. I am indebted to the late G. C. E. V. Evans, Esq., formerly the owner of Aberglasney, and to Mrs. Evans, now Mrs. Lyndon Skeggs, for allowing photostats of the verses to be made and for permission to print the poem here.

[31] Willmott, p. 2. See also Richard C. Boys, ed., *Grongar Hill by John Dyer* (Baltimore, 1941), p. 45.

poetry; as Longstaffe points out,[32] the legal expression "felon fraud" in *The Fleece* (I. 143) is the only survival of the law in his poems.

John Dyer's apprenticeship to the law came to an end, however, after the death of his father on July 8, 1720.[33] Robert Dyer the younger, who was named executor of his father's will, was in London at the time and did not return to Aberglasney for several months, so that the preliminary details of settling the estate fell upon John Dyer and Howell Williams.[34] In his will, after providing adequately for his wife, the elder Dyer left to his son Robert the Lordship and Priory of Kidwelly and all his property in the parishes of Llanddarog and Llanvihangel Rhos Y Corn, for the better paying of his debts and mortgages.[35] He bequeathed six hundred pounds to his son John, four hundred to his son Thomas, and six hundred to his son Bennet, to be paid on their twenty-fourth birthdays with interest from the date of his death. The rest of his property he devised for ten years to his business associates, William Robert and Thomas Thomas, to collect the rents therefrom and apply them to paying off the mortgages on the land. This property, including Aberglasney, Robert Dyer, Sr. entailed in the male line of the family—an

---

[32] *Collations and Additions to the Poems of John Dyer, L.L.B.*, the notes which Longstaffe sent instead of the manuscripts to Willmott for the latter's edition of Dyer. This is one of the notes which Willmott omitted.

[33] The exact date is given in Lloyd vs. Dyer, P.R.O., C.11.995/14 and Dyer vs. Dyer, P.R.O., C.33.349, fol. 504 verso. He was buried in Llangathen July 12 (Green, p. 101).

[34] Woodroffe vs. Dyer, P.R.O., C.11.1022/27. The elder Dyer's will was dated May 16 and proved Nov. 22, 1720. It is now at Somerset House, London.

[35] This was a wise precaution; at his death the elder Dyer's debts chargeable to his personal estate (as opposed to mortgages on real estate) amounted to £2197/14/6, or over £1000 more than the assets of his personal estate. He also owed £4050 plus interest on real estate, but his property was more than enough to meet these demands in the plan outlined in his will.

entail which a descendant of Thomas Dyer seriously considered trying to enforce late in the nineteenth century![36]

The elder Dyer's estate was not in very good order when he died and caused his sons trouble for the next ten years in lawsuits—a legacy not mentioned in the will. But otherwise, with the return of his brother to Aberglasney to manage their father's estate, John Dyer was free to follow whatever profession he chose. Late in 1720 or in 1721 he went to London to study painting.

[36] Letters of Charles Henry Dyer to his distant cousin, W. H. D. Longstaffe, now in the possession of Longstaffe's grandson, Ronald Hylton Smith, Esq., of Cottingham, Yorks.

CHAPTER II

"Painting Fair the Form of Things"

At his arrival in London Dyer began the study of painting
with the well-known artist Jonathan Richardson, who was perhaps even then, as Johnson said of him later, "better known by
his books than by his pictures." [1] Richardson, however, was
much more than just a theorist about the art of painting. Samuel Redgrave says that Richardson had a good reputation as a
portrait painter even during the lives of Kneller and Dahl, and
that after their deaths he ranked with Jervas at the head of his
profession. [2] Matthew Pilkington says that he had no equal as
a portrayer of heads, although the rest of his work was not so
good. [3] Dyer too admired his instructor's painting, and they seem
to have been excellent friends. In his "Epistle to a Famous
Painter," obviously addressed to Richardson, [4] Dyer speaks of
him as the

> Delightful partner of my heart,
> Master of the loveliest art!

One of Richardson's fundamental precepts was that an
artist's life was intimately related to the quality of his work:
his reading, his observation of nature, his study of the work of
the masters in painting, his writing of poetry, and his associa-

---

[1] Johnson's *Lives*, III, 343.

[2] Samuel Redgrave, *Dictionary of Artists of the English School*
(London, 1874), p. 339.

[3] M[atthew] Pilkington, *A Dictionary of Painters*, rev. by Henry
Fuseli (London, 1805), p. 450.

[4] I should note, however, that Christopher Hussey, in *The Picturesque* (London, 1927), p. 39, says that it "is apparently a post-
humous one [epistle] to Claude."

tion with the brightest company available, all should supply his mind with noble images, with original ideas of grace and greatness.[5] Under Richardson's influence Dyer began to read widely and to make commonplace books on his reading. One of these was entitled "Plans for the Studies of Arts and Sciences" (Richardson emphasized the need of a painter to know his sciences well[6]), and others were volumes of quotations on proportion, collections on terms in painting, and subjects for painting.[7] Apparently the only one of these notebooks to survive to the present, however, is the one entitled by Longstaffe "Early Extracts from the Poets and the Bible." The passages in this book were selected for two or three different reasons and point up several of Dyer's lasting interests.[8] Quotations appealing to one or more of the senses abound. Those creating visual images could well have been selected as subjects for painting; a typical example (one that Dyer copied out twice in this one notebook) is from *Paradise Lost,* comparing the fallen angels to trees struck by lightning:

> yet faithful how they stood,
> Their glory withered. As when Heaven's fire
> Hath scathed the forest oaks, or mountain pines,
> With singed top their stately growth though bare
> Stands on the blasted heath.   (I. 611-5)

Other passages were selected probably as being suitable for poetry—either as ideas for whole poems, or figures of speech to be

---

[5] [Jonathan] Richardson, *An Essay on the Theory of Painting* (London, 1715), pp. 190-213, esp. 190-1, 197-9.

[6] Richardson, p. 22.

[7] *Montgomeryshire Collections,* XI (London, 1878), 400-401.

[8] Over half the pages of this long notebook (136 pp. remain) are filled with quotations from *Paradise Lost;* a sixth, roughly, come from Spenser (*The Faerie Queene* and *Virgil's Gnat*), and another sixth from the Bible (Old Testament and Apocrypha only). Blank pages and miscellaneous notes and meditations account for the remaining pages. This is the notebook we have lettered D (see Foreword).

imitated, or poetic words and phrases to be used. One page is devoted entirely to three columns of very Miltonic words ("alterne," "disparted," "whelms," etc.), some of which were apparently strange enough to Dyer to make him write in the meaning too. Selections describing trees or cascades of water are his two most obvious favorites, reflecting his fondness at this time for descriptive poetry and (probably) for landscape painting.

Although Dyer's sketch books have disappeared, his notebooks show that his enjoyment of nature continued as great as when he was living regularly at Aberglasney. And although his only extant copies of the works of the masters date from his visit to Italy in 1724-5, he had a wonderful opportunity to study their work in the fine collection of drawings and paintings amassed by Richardson. Apparently Richardson also urged his students to go out sketching interesting examples of architecture, picturesque scenes, and other suitable objects. Sometime before the death of the first Duke of Marlborough in July, 1722, for example, Dyer visited Blenheim Palace and saw the famous tapestries there which he later described in *The Fleece*.[9] In his "Early Extracts from the Poets and the Bible" he mentions several picturesque spots in Wales: the "cascade a little above New Radnor" (possibly the famous waterfall known as "Water-break-itsneck") he could have seen without too much trouble going to or from Aberglasney, but Chirk Castle, near Llangollen, Denbighshire, the Devil's Bridge in Cardiganshire, and Trevernon,

---

[9] III. 498-517. Among his unpublished mss. is a quatrain entitled "At the Sight of the D[uke] of M[arlborough], who was helpless and thought an Idiot before he died":

> Marlbrough behold, victorious! first of men!
> Proud are we now of life? Behold again
> Yon feeble idiot in the lonely dome,
> Marlbrough the lowest of his kind become.

Mr. Sacre, the present land agent at Blenheim, informs me that there are no paintings by Dyer there, so his visit was probably for the purpose of sketching the palace which the nation had built for its great general.

LANDSCAPE BY DYER

The foreground is very sombre, done largely in shades of brown which do
not reproduce well. The small patch of yellow sunshine in the distance shows
the influence of the Italian landscape artists of the 17th century (see Elizabeth
W. Manwaring, *Italian Landscape in Eighteenth Century England*, New York,
1925). The painting now belongs to Ronald Hylton Smith, Esq.

an estate belonging to a Colonel Owens in Merionethshire "by the sea side," would have involved a special trip into North Wales. North Wales was a favorite area with Dyer, and although the earliest tour of his there which we can date was in 1728, there is no reason for believing that these notes do not apply to a trip planned and probably made before Dyer went to Italy. And it may have been at this time that he went to Canterbury, where, he wrote William Duncombe in 1757, he had visited.[10]

Richardson also believed that the painter must "have the talents requisite to a good poet, the rules for the conduct of a picture being much the same with those to be observed in writing a poem."[11] This idea, a common one at the time, obviously encouraged Dyer to continue with the writing of poetry, an art in which he considered himself more proficient than in painting at this time, for in his "Epistle to a Famous Painter" he wrote:

> To me reveal thy heavenly art,
> To me thy mysteries impart.
> As yet I but in verse can paint.   (18-20)

Richardson was a great admirer of Milton, and as this poem is probably Dyer's first attempt to use the octo-syllabic couplets of Milton's "L'Allegro" and "Il Penseroso," it is perhaps not conjecturing too much to suggest that Dyer's interest in this meter was aroused by his instructor in painting.

But most important of all was his frequenting "the brightest company,"[12] and it will be with Dyer's friends, consequently, that most of the remainder of this chapter will be concerned. Dyer came from what was considered a "good" family, and had "connections" which were the envy of at least one of his literary friends.[13] He probably lived in the vicinity of Lincoln's Inn

---

[10] Duncombe's *Letters*, III, 68.

[11] Richardson, p. 21.

[12] Richardson, p. 191.

[13] Richard Savage. His exchange of poems with Dyer on this point will be discussed later in this chapter.

Fields, then a favorite resort of artists as well as lawyers, and the residence of Richardson.[14] As he had not yet received his inheritance from his father's estate, he presumably lived on an allowance given him by his family. He would, therefore, have to live modestly, but he was able, apparently, to return to Aberglasney in the summer, go on sketching trips out from London, and call at his favorite coffee house daily and there meet and talk with the other young artists and law students who lived in the neighborhood. His friends at this time of whom we know fall into three or four groups, which I shall take up one by one.

At the time that Dyer was studying with him, Richardson had at least two other pupils, Thomas Hudson and George Knapton. Hudson, later one of Richardson's sons-in-law, is today primarily remembered as the instructor of Sir Joshua Reynolds. Knapton, although less famous than Hudson, is more important to us since it was apparently through him that Dyer met many of his best friends, especially the group which congregated at Serle's Coffee House, in Carey Street, near Serle's Gate, leading from the New Court of Lincoln's Inn to Carey Street.

Serle's was not one of the famous coffee houses of the eighteenth century, but it was popular with the students at Lincoln's Inn, and was used as an example by Steele in his satire on the vanity and affectations of law students in coffee houses.[15] One of Dyer's friends, Thomas Edwards, although not typical of the "vain things" described by Steele, did ask one of his correspondents to send mail to Serle's Coffee House because he went there every morning,[16] and others may have done likewise, for as Steele said, "The coffee house is the place of rendezvous to all that live near it."

Dyer's closest friends in this group at Serle's were Thomas Edwards and Daniel Wray, who had been boyhood friends in

---

[14] Duncombe's *Letters,* III, 61; *The Poetical Works of Armstrong, Dyer and Green,* ed. George Gilfillan (Edinburgh, 1868), p. 101.

[15] *The Spectator,* no. 49.

[16] Ms. Bodl. 1007, p. 8.

Essex.[17] Edwards was at this time living at Number 8, Lincoln's Inn New Square,[18] although frequently visiting his family estate, Pitshanger, near Acton, Essex. His love of literature later found expression in his very clever satire, *The Canons of Criticism,* and in helping to revive the sonnet; at this time it found satisfaction in talking and versifying with friends of similar interests. And, what is perhaps more pertinent to our immediate purpose, he was keeping letter books, that is, notebooks in which he copied many (though not all) of his letters, from which we get a very good picture of this group.[19] Daniel Wray was at Queens' College, Cambridge, receiving his bachelor's degree in 1722 and his master's in 1728, but he visited London frequently enough to take a part in the activities of these young men, especially after 1722.

Two other friends at Serle's, George Knapton and Arthur Pond, are best remembered today for their collaboration in publishing a series of drawings from eminent masters. Knapton is mentioned frequently in Edwards' letters, and as he was studying with Richardson at this time, he seems the most likely person to have introduced Dyer to this group. Pond is generally said to have been born about 1705, but must have been born somewhat earlier, and like the rest of these friends, within a year or two of the turn of the century. He either leased or owned a house in Great Queen's Street, near Lincoln's Inn Fields, letting the extra rooms, and here at one time or another Dyer, Edwards, and Wray later took lodgings. Pond was well known as a collector of drawings and curiosities, and it is in this capacity that he appears in *The Fleece* (IV. 265). And there were others whom

---

[17] See Edwards' sonnet to Wray in *The Canons of Criticism* (6th ed., London, 1758), p. 292 or in *A Collection of Poems in Six Volumes by Several Hands,* ed. [Robert Dodsley] (5th ed., London, 1758), II, 333. Wray's father, Sir Daniel Wray, Knt., owned an estate near Ingatestone, Essex, not far from Pitshanger.

[18] Ms. Bodl. 1007, p. 10.

[19] Now in the Bodleian Library, Oxford, as Mss. Bodl. 1007-1012.

Dyer probably knew also and who appear frequently in Edwards' letters: Lewis Crusius, whose *Lives of the Roman Poets* Dyer later read and quoted from in his notebooks, and whom he may have visited in Herefordshire;[20] George Knapton's brother, Charles, an engraver; and John Forster, to whom Edwards quoted *The Ruins of Rome* as by an old friend.[21]

Every coffee house presumably had its club or clubs, growing out of small groups of men who habitually met together there, and Serle's was no exception. On January 1, 1722/3, Edwards wrote to Wray (then in Cambridge):

> In the meantime, as you know, we have instituted a club, "Quod felix faustumque sit" etc. I take the liberty of sending you a *petite chançon* which was communicated to us: "To Florella"[22] We are as yet but in our infancy but we hope in time to render ourselves considerable in the commonwealth of wit and letters, especially when we can have the happiness of your assistance.
>
> From as small beginnings as these have risen societies whose names are handed down to posterity with honour, and who knows but this may be the foundation of a glorious building.[23]

The club does not appear frequently in Edwards' letters, and was disrupted in 1724 by the removal of much of its membership

---

[20] Crusius was chaplain to Lord Bateman and rector of Shobden, Herefordshire. Dyer gives a brief description of the famous terrace at Shobden in *The Fleece,* I. 55-8.

[21] John Forster spent most of his life in India, where Edwards and Wray annually sent him a joint letter and parcel of books. The quotation occurs in their letter of Oct. 26, 1741 (Ms. Bodl. 1009, p. 193).

[22] Unfortunately Edwards did not copy the entire poem into his letter book. He sent a poem with this title to his friend Henry Travers for Travers' *Miscellaneous Poems and Translations* (London, 1731), but it was not included (Ms. Bodl. 1007, p. 87). A poem "On Florella's Birthday" appears in Stephen Duck's *Poems on Several Occasions* (London, 1736), pp. 158-9; there seems to be no evidence, however, that it is by Edwards or that it was one of the poems which caused some trouble in 1732 (see below).

[23] Ms. Bodl. 1007, pp. 36-7.

to Italy before its high ideals could be realized. That its members were versifying at this time, however, is suggested, I think, by the consternation shown by Edwards and Wray in 1732 when they learned that some of their early verses had been given by a "female friend" of theirs to Stephen Duck for a miscellany he was then preparing.[24]

Dyer was associated, however, with a group which did manage to render itself "considerable in the commonwealth of wit and letters"—in fact, with what was probably the most considerable literary group in London in the early 1720's, the circle gathered around Aaron Hill. The members, thoughts, and activities of this society have been so well described by Professor Brewster,[25] that all I need do here is emphasize Dyer's relations with some of his closer friends.

As the ladies played a much more active part in this group, its gatherings were held not in a coffee house, but in the homes of the members, particularly the Hills' and Clio's.[26] Much of the activity seems to have been tea drinking and a sort of Platonic gallantry inspired by pastoral romances. Twenty years later Benjamin Victor, writing to Dyer and recalling these times, said, "How many delightful hours have we enjoyed with that elegant lover [Hill] and his charming Clio! how like those scenes we read in our youthful days in Sir Philip Sidney's pastoral romance!" [27]

"Clio" was the poetic name used by Mrs. Martha Fowke Sansom in signing her verses and in playing the combined roles of Pamela and Philoclea in this romantic gallantry. She was

---

[24] Ms. Bodl. 1007, pp. 194-5, 198.

[25] Dorothy Brewster, *Aaron Hill, Poet, Dramatist, Projector* (New York, 1913), Chapter V, "Hill and His Circle about 1725," pp. 153-200.

[26] Brewster, p. 172; "To Aaron Hill, Esq.," in *Poems on Several Occasions,* by Joseph Mitchell, 2 vols. (London, 1729), I, 312; David Mallet to John Ker, Feb. 21, 1725/6, in *The European Magazine,* XXIV (London, 1793), 258.

[27] Benjamin Victor, *Original Letters, Dramatic Pieces, and Poems* (London, 1776), I, 68.

probably neither as virtuous as her autobiography portrays her,[28] nor as wicked as the picture drawn of her by her arch-enemy, Mrs. Eliza Haywood.[29] There is little doubt, however, that she was a beautiful and charming lady, to whom all the men in the group were expected to offer themselves as servants and to direct amatory verses in praise of her beauty. Although Hill was her most "elegant lover," Dyer, Savage, Mallet and others wrote verses to her.

But Dyer, "Whose verse and pencil join to force reward," as Clio said,[30] had something else to offer. During the winter of 1723-4, he painted her portrait.[31] His friends in this coterie already admired his painting, but to portray Clio seemed to be undertaking the impossible. They all showed great interest in the project; Hill wrote a poem on the picture while it was being painted, as did Savage and Clio herself after it was completed.[32] To praise Dyer's skill as a painter became practically a second convention of this group.

Dyer's relations with Clio were thoroughly misunderstood by his descendant Longstaffe, who was convinced that John was deeply enamored of this lady, and Willmott, whom Longstaffe

---

[28] [Martha Fowke Sansom,] *Clio: or, a Secret History of the Life and Amours of the late celebrated Mrs. S---n---m*. Written by Herself in a letter to Hillarius [Aaron Hill]. (Dated Oct., 1723, at the end of the text, but apparently first published in London in 1752.)

[29] Eliza Haywood, *Memoirs of a Certain Island Adjacent to the Kingdom of Utopia* (2nd ed., 1726), I, 43-9, 183-4, 291-3.

[30] [Martha Fowke Sansom,] "To Mr. John Dyer," Savage's *Miscellany*, p. 210.

[31] In her autobiography dated Oct., 1723, Clio records sitting for her portrait only once, to one C---y (p. 103). In Hill's periodical, *The Plain Dealer*, for May 11, 1724 (2nd collected ed. [London, 1734], I, 115-6) appeared Savage's poem to Dyer on the completed picture.

[32] Savage's *Miscellany*, pp. 26-30, 58-9, 209-10. It is interesting that both Hill and Savage stress Dyer's ability at heroic painting, for no pictures of his in that style have survived. Most of his extant paintings are portraits or landscapes.

provided with all the material for his edition of Dyer's works, made this opinion general.[33] Dyer, along with the other men, did write verses to Clio, but Longstaffe interpreted them much too literally, not realizing that in the poetic effusions of this group it was taken for granted that Clio's beauty should be praised. Longstaffe was further misled by a change in Clio's poetic name, and argued that Dyer, having been jilted by Clio, began to address his verses to Mira out of spite. In his poem, "The Happy Disappointment," for example, after telling of his mistake in making advances to a certain lady, Dyer returns to the comforting thought that "Mira shall be kind."[34] Mira, however, was none other than Clio; in 1726 the name had become so abused by poetical imitators and scandal-mongers that Mrs. Sansom found it convenient to adopt some other *non de plume,* and was renamed Mira by David Mallet.[35] And Clio herself, in her poem,

---

[33] As an illustration I quote from an article on "James Thomson and David Mallet," in *The Athenaeum,* XXXII, part ii (London, 1859), 78: "Poor John Dyer, the simple author of 'Grongar Hill,' appears to have fallen for a time hopelessly into the power of the syren Clio, and is sighing and dying about her in most of his short poems. Mr. Willmott, who, in his pleasing sketch of Dyer, also speculates on the lady's identity, is puzzled at finding how rapidly Mira, not Clio, becomes the object of the poet's idolatry."

[34] *The Patrician,* IV (1847), 425; Willmott does not give the text of the poem, but refers to it on p. xii. Longstaffe, it should be noted, says that Mira was a "Mrs. G---r," but it seems unlikely that Dyer would use the same poetic name for two friends, and Longstaffe was capable of misreading what Dyer wrote in his marginal notes.

[35] *The British Journal,* no. 210 (Sept. 24, 1726): "Clio must be allowed to be a most complete poetess, if she really wrote those poems that bear her name; but it has of late been so abused and scandalized, that I am informed she has lately changed it for that of Myra; and that a dapper Scotch gentleman [Mallet], the author of the two last poems in the [Savage's] Miscellany (and an admirer, as appears by the first copy) was the first that new-christened her." Quoted by Peter Cunningham, "James Thomson and David Mallet," *Miscellanies* of the Philobiblon Society, IV (1858), 12n.

"My Last Will. To the Immortal Hillarius [Aaron Hill]," indicates that Dyer was not one of her ardent lovers:

> But lest this heavenly cordial may decline
> Let me present thy soul with one of mine;
> Next to thyself most noble and sincere,
> The[36] second jewel in my journey here.
> Oh! let me recommend him to thy care,
> To soften pains, and make misfortunes fair.
> Can I a nobler character impart?
> Oh place this blessing in thy godlike heart!
> He knew my passion [for Hill], and he sweetly knew
> To keep its brightness, yet to soothe it too;
> His youth and undesigning breast defend,
> And wear to death itself this valued friend.
> No more, what have I else entitled mine,
> My life, my soul, my muse, my friend, are thine.[37]

Another character whom Victor mentioned in his letter of reminiscence was Richard Savage. Victor was writing when Dr. Johnson was preparing his life of Savage, and recommended that Johnson, if he "would enrich and enliven his work . . . should come to you, and I, for anecdotes," suggesting that he and Dyer had known Savage very well.[38] Savage's famous story of his descent from the Earl Rivers and the Countess of Macclesfield has made him a fascinating figure for biographers and novelists ever since Johnson's time, and it is a temptation to deal with his origins here, but they have been well discussed by Moy Thomas in *Notes and Queries* and more recently by Professor C. R. Tracy in his study of Savage.[39] In justice to Dyer, Hill, and others who may have believed his tale, however, it should be remembered that even though they did not have access to the records of the

---

[36] "Mr. John D--r."—Clio's note.

[37] [Sansom,] *Clio,* pp. 206-7.

[38] Victor, *Original Letters,* I, 68.

[39] *N&Q,* 2nd series, VI (Nov. 6, 13, 27, Dec. 4, 1858), 361-5, 385-9, 425-8, 445-8; Clarence Tracy, *The Artificial Bastard* (Cambridge, Mass., 1953), pp. 3-27.

divorce trial of the Earl and Countess of Macclesfield (as have Moy Thomas and other modern scholars), they may have had sources of information closed to us today. Dyer's friend David Lewis, for example, was the son-in-law of Newdigate Ousley,[40] the agent of the Earl Rivers in all his dealings with the Countess of Macclesfield, and the man to whom, Moy Thomas believes, their real son was entrusted when their intrigue was discovered —the point at which the child disappears from the records of reliable history.[41]

Of Savage's poverty and need of assistance, however, there can be no doubt. Johnson says that during the winter of 1723-4, when Savage was working on *The Tragedy of Sir Thomas Overbury,* "he was without lodging, and often without meat; nor had he any other conveniences for study than the fields or the street allowed him: there he used to walk and form his speeches, and afterwards step into a shop, beg for a few moments the use of the pen and ink, and write down what he had composed upon paper which he had picked up by accident." [42] Hill helped Savage with the play, which proved quite successful and brought Savage some hundred pounds from all sources. Similarly everyone in the group helped him with the *Miscellany* he was then preparing. Dyer contributed six poems to it, and, as did the others, subscribed for the volume.

Apparently Savage felt, however, that there was more that Dyer might do for him. Savage's verses in the fifteenth *Plain Dealer,* especially if read in the context of the essay which precedes them, are obviously not merely a suggestion that Dyer paint great Horatius, but a strong hint that Horatius become the patron of Savage, presumably through having Dyer introduce them.[43] Dyer's reply is comforting though vague, assuring Savage

---

[40] G. F. Russell Barker, *The Record of Old Westminsters* (London, 1928), II, 575; *N&Q,* 2nd series, VI, 426.

[41] *N&Q,* 2nd series, VI (Nov. 27, 1858), 365.

[42] Johnson's *Lives,* II, 338-9.

[43] *The Plain Dealer,* no. 15 (2nd collected ed., London, 1734), I, 111-6, esp. the words of "the Major" to Hill on p. 114: "Who-

that even though popular acclaim may not be his, the "truly great" admire him and his verse.[44]   Savage acknowledges the comfort, but continues by saying that Dyer has misunderstood him; he has ambitions beyond the literary:

> Think not light poetry, my life's chief care,
> The Muse's mansion is at best but air!
> Not sounding verse can give great souls their aim,
> Action alone commands substantial fame.[45]

And it is in the realm of *action* that his scope is contracted by not having a patron.

The exchange of poems had been completed before the first one was printed in the *Plain Dealer* on May 11, 1724; Savage's second one implies that it was written at the time of "the opening spring." [46] But sometime in April before the second of Savage's poems was written, Dyer had gone back to Aberglasney, for these verses were addressed to him "when in the country." Later in the year he set out for Italy, perhaps without returning to London, so that at this time Savage's hint bore no fruit, although it may have later.

One cannot help but wonder what Dyer's feelings were towards Hill for printing Savage's first poem and supporting it as obviously as he did in his introduction in the *Plain Dealer*. The publication suggests that presentation to Dyer in manuscript form had not been effective; Dyer's poem certainly is one of encourage-

---

ever may be meant by Horatius, if he makes as handsome a figure in his reception of the poet [Savage], as he does in the poet's description, he will be to him instead of a Maecenas; and you [Hill] will have the satisfaction of knowing that you put the meritorious in a way to meet reward and administer an opportunity, the most grateful that can be to a person truly great, an opportunity of doing a graceful action."

[44] Savage's *Miscellany*, pp. 291-3.

[45] Savage's *Miscellany*, p. 295.

[46] It is said to have been "Written in the Month of April" when republished by Savage twelve years later in the *GM*, VI (1736), 743, and in the *London Magazine*, V (1736), 693.

ment, not a promise of help. Perhaps Savage and Hill hoped to
point out more clearly to Dyer what they meant and at the same
time make it possible for some potential patron to read the poem
in the *Plain Dealer* and see himself in the portrait of Horatius.
Or they may have had a definite person in mind by this time,
as I shall presently suggest, even though originally Horatius may
well have been a generalized portrait. In any case Dyer's relationship with Hill was different from that of most of the other
members of the group in that Dyer was not in need of Hill's
help and patronage as were Savage, Bond, Mitchell, Mallet,
and, later on, even Thomson. Yet Dyer took part fully in the
conventional gallantry of the group, including the flattery of Hill
as a poet and lover; there is no less adulation in Dyer's verses
on Hill's *Gideon* than in Savage's poem on the same subject.[47]
And on the other hand Hill was just as extravagant when he
wrote of Dyer:

> Soul of your honour'd art!—What man can do
> In copying nature, may be reached by you.[48]

A third group of friends grew up, I think, out of the fact
that Dyer's father had served as land agent and solicitor for
Charles Seymour, sixth Duke of Somerset, commonly known as
"the proud Duke." When Robert Dyer, Sr. died, he owed His
Grace over three hundred pounds,[49] and perhaps in settling his
father's estate John undertook to pay this debt in person—possibly at Marlborough on his way to London. In some way, at
any rate, Dyer became acquainted with the Duke of Somerset's
daughter-in-law, Lady Hertford, and became one of the poets
whom she was fond of entertaining at Marlborough.

The evidence for Dyer's friendship with Lady Hertford is
preserved in one of her commonplace books, into which she has

---

[47] Savage's *Miscellany,* pp. 117-21, 205-8.

[48] Savage's *Miscellany,* p. 58.

[49] P.R.O., C.11.1022/27. For an account of this lawsuit, see my
article, "Robert Dyer the Elder of Aberglasney, Gent.," *The Carmarthen Antiquary,* II (1951), 75-88.

copied two of Dyer's poems.[50] One of these, Dyer's verses to Thomson, is unique; the other, the second version of *Grongar Hill,* is otherwise known only through the *New Miscellany,* published early in 1726.[51] A number of poems in the *New Miscellany* (a hastily put together and piratical volume of poems collected at various watering places during the winter of 1725-6) seem to have Lady Hertford as their ultimate origin.[52] It is natural to assume, therefore, that *Grongar Hill* too reached Warner, the publisher, directly or indirectly from Lady Hertford, and that she therefore had the poem by the end of 1725.

How and when she got the poem is of some interest to conjecture. Dyer could, of course, have sent it to her by post, but as she was in the habit of inviting poets to visit her at Marlborough, particularly in the summer, I am inclined to believe that Dyer was entertained by her and gave her the poem himself. This was probably before his trip to Italy, for upon his return in the summer of 1725, as we shall see, he went directly to his family in Carmarthenshire, and by that autumn surely he must have had ready the third version of *Grongar Hill,* which appeared in David Lewis' *Miscellany* at about the same time that the *New Miscellany* was published. The earliest, or Pindaric ode version of *Grongar Hill* appeared in Savage's *Miscellany* which, according to the *Plain Dealer* for November 30, 1724, was then

---

[50] Alnwick Ms. 116, pp. 4-9, 114-5. I am very grateful to His Grace, the late Duke of Northumberland, for giving me permission to inspect Lady Hertford's papers at Alnwick Castle. The two poems have been published by Professor Helen Sard Hughes, "John Dyer and the Countess of Hertford," *Mod. Phil.,* XXVII (1930), 311-20.

[51] A. D. McKillop, reviewing *Grongar Hill,* by John Dyer, ed. Richard C. Boys (Baltimore, 1941), in *MLN,* LVII (1942), 481-2.

[52] For example, Laurence Eusden's poem, "On the Countess of H-rtf-rd" (p. 14) and Lady Hertford's own compositions, "The Story of Inkle and Yarico" (pp. 32-7) and "An Epistle from Yarico to Inkle" (pp. 38-41). See also Helen Sard Hughes, *The Gentle Hertford* (New York, 1940), pp. 419-21.

ready for the press.[53] It seems probable to me, therefore, that
Dyer was a guest at Marlborough during the summer of 1724,
perhaps on his way to Carmarthenshire.[54]

All this brings us back to Dyer's exchange of poems with
Savage. I should like to suggest that Horatius, whom Dyer was
advised to paint, was the Duke of Somerset, in whose palatial
residence he would soon be visiting. Savage described His Grace
exactly,[55] and probably wrote with a full knowledge that Dyer
intended to visit Marlborough soon; like many of Savage's poems,
it was well timed. And some point to the publication of the
poem in the *Plain Dealer* thus appears also—Savage may have
asked Hill to print it in the hope that it would be seen at Marlborough and Dyer recognized as the painter, and so any reticence
on the latter's part be overcome. There is no evidence that the
Duke of Somerset ever accepted the role of Horatius and patron-

---

[53] *The Plain Dealer,* no. 73 (2nd collected ed., London, 1734),
II, 138-40. Savage's statement (p. 140), "The book is now in the
press, and will be published as soon as it can be printed off," is no
doubt an exaggeration, but his friends probably had given him
enough poems by this time "to furnish out a collection of Miscellaneous Poems," as he says earlier (p. 138). "A Poem on the Recovery of her Grace the Dutchess of Rutland from Small-Pox"
(Savage's *Miscellany,* pp. 1-4) and "The Animalcule, a Tale; occasioned by the Inoculation of the Duke of Rutland" (*ibid.,* pp.
129-34) both celebrate events which occurred in April, 1725. See
Tracy, *The Artificial Bastard,* p. 65.

[54] The usual route from London to South Wales in the 18th
century was the Oxford, Gloucester, and Milford Haven road. But
if one did not mind ferrying across the lower Severn near Bristol,
the Bath and Bristol road (on which Marlborough was situated)
was quite as satisfactory.

[55] *The Plain Dealer,* no. 15 (2nd collected ed., London, 1734),
I, 116, and Savage's *Miscellany,* p. 29. In the *Miscellany* the description of Horatius has been expanded by six lines and made more
specific—and more like the "proud Duke." For accounts of the
Duke of Somerset, see the *DNB* and the good short one in Arthur
Collins, *The Peerage of England* (5th ed., London, 1779), I, 168-
71.

ized Savage, but Johnson reports that in 1727, when Savage was under sentence of death for murder, it was through the efforts of the Countess of Hertford that a pardon from the Queen was obtained for the poet.[56]

Much of the last two paragraphs has, of necessity, been conjectural, but we may accept the fact that Dyer was well acquainted with Lady Hertford and probably, like his friend James Thomson, returned on more than one occasion to Marlborough. Whom of the other literary figures who were acquainted with Lady Hertford he knew, it is impossible to say today, but that the company at Marlborough met Richardson's standards for a good painter we may, I think, be sure.

Dyer's fourth set of friends was, rather surprisingly, carried over from Westminster days. Even though he had been unhappy at the school at first, Dyer seems to have made some lasting friendships there. This group centered around David Lewis, who had attended Westminster and the Middle Temple. As a man of law he had had some business with Dyer's father.[57] Ultimately he returned to Westminster as an usher and there edited his well known miscellany, the first volume of which appeared in 1726. In the Preface to this volume he says:

I have received my chiefest assistance from a set of gentlemen of both universities now in London . . . I shall add no more than to wish, which I have no reason to mistrust, that the world may be as well pleas'd with the good sense and ingenuity of their writing, as I am happy in their conversation and friendship.[58]

Dyer, although not of a university as yet, was one of this "set," which included Samuel Wesley the younger, the Latin poet Vin-

---

[56] Johnson's *Lives,* II, 352. I should add that Professor Tracy, with whom I have discussed the question, does not agree with my interpretation; cf. Clarence Tracy, *The Artificial Bastard* (Cambridge, Mass., 1953), pp. 68-72.

[57] P.R.O., C.11.1022/27.

[58] Lewis' *Miscellany,* I (London, 1726), leaf A4 verso.

cent Bourne, and others whom I shall mention when I come to
discuss Lewis' *Miscellany* itself.

During these years of literary and artistic activity, Dyer was
not entirely free of the law, for in 1722 he was named one of
the defendants in a lawsuit rising out of the right of redemption
of certain property, which right his father had purchased in
1717.[59] Because of the death of various principals, the right had
become involved, and so the parties concerned, in a friendly
fashion,[60] brought the case before the Court of Chancery to be
straightened out. John Dyer's answer to the bill of complaint is
dated April 2, 1724,[61] indicating that he had not left London
by then at any rate. And he was already planning for his trip
to Italy, for in this reply he asks the Court to provide, amongst
other things, for the payment of the six hundred pounds left him
by his father which was now due, as he had reached his twenty-
fourth birthday. That he should include such a recommendation
in his answer suggests that he had already asked his older brother
for the sum, presumably to finance his journey, and had been
put off.

Richardson's program of reading and writing, study and companionship, was well designed, I think, to bring out the best in
John Dyer. It stimulated his imagination enough to appeal to
the artist in him, and was practical and specific enough to appeal
to him as a man of affairs. The six or seven poems from this
period which have survived all show a great advancement on
Dyer's part in the technique of verse writing, and some, such as
"The Country Walk," are among the best of all his compositions.
Much practice must have intervened between his juvenile verses
and these more finished products, but he had the good sense,

---

[59] P.R.O., C.11.995/14; C.11.996/5; C.11.1001/18; C.11.1229/
41 & 43; C.33.342, fol. 11a; C.33.344, fol. 302b. I have outlined
the lawsuit quite fully in my article, "The Dyer Family of Aberglasney," *The Carmarthen Antiquary,* I (1941), 30-42.

[60] For example, Mrs. Grace Lloyd, one of the plaintiffs, later
became the wife of Bennet Dyer, one of the defendants.

[61] P.R.O., C.11.995/14.

apparently, to destroy the results of such practice. Although none of his paintings which are known can be assigned to this period, no doubt his work in this medium had matured and developed as had his poetry.

CHAPTER III

"Of Proud Antiquity"

Although Dyer enjoyed and appreciated the praises of his
friends on his painting, he was too good a critic of himself to
be satisfied with the progress he was making, and consequently
in 1724 he decided to continue his studies in Italy. Several circumstances probably helped him to make this decision at this
time. He was past his twenty-fourth birthday, when his legacy
from his father came due, and he apparently hoped his brother
would pay him his £600 to finance his expedition; George
Knapton, Arthur Pond, Daniel Wray, and perhaps others of his
friends were going to Italy at this time; and most important of
all, he had probably reached a stage in his development at which
Richardson felt that the travel abroad would do his painting the
most good.

Actually, however, Robert Dyer did not pay John his £600
until 1729. Once again, John showed his independence of mind
by determining to go to Italy in 1724 anyway, not when it proved
convenient for his brother to raise the sum he owed him. This
meant, then, that he had to finance his trip with the allowance
his family gave him, and though that may have done handsomely
for living in London, it was quite inadequate for a tour of Italy.
He showed the thinness of his pocketbook at the very outset by
choosing to go to Italy entirely by sea. Mead says that in the
eighteenth century "comparatively few made the long voyage
through the Straits of Gibraltar to Italy. And it was well that
they did not. The ships were commonly small and dirty, the
food bad, the weather often rough." [1] Dyer apparently left no
record of the cleanliness of his ship or the quality of the food,

---

[1] William Edward Mead, *The Grand Tour in the Eighteenth
Century* (Boston, 1914), pp. 142-3.

but he did experience the smallness of the ship and the rough-
ness of the weather, for in his "Journal of Escapes" he wrote,
"1724. Narrow escape in a storm at Calwater, 1 of Plymouth
harbours, in my voyage to Italy." [2] This seems to have been no
uncommon experience; the *British Journal* for March 14, 1723/4
reports: "They write from Falmouth of the 9th instant, that the
Boscowen Packet, bound for Lisbon, was forced back thither by
contrary winds, having lost her masts." [3] Dyer was still in England in April, 1724, as we have seen, but it was no doubt some
similar accident that occurred at the beginning of his voyage.

Dyer probably stopped at Lisbon and one or two other
points and then disembarked at Leghorn, an important English
trading center with a sizable English colony. Mead says that
"constant communication with England made Leghorn a convenient port of entry and departure for those English tourists
who did not object to a long sea voyage. And since at Leghorn
they found many of the inhabitants speaking English tolerably
well, they felt at once at home." [4]

Immediately upon landing Dyer wrote to his family and
then, probably fairly rapidly, went down the west side of Italy

---

[2] *The Patrician,* IV (1847), 265.

[3] *The British Journal,* no. 78 (March 14, 1723/4), p. 5, col. 2.

[4] Mead, p. 307. Dyer may even have found friends in Leghorn
when he arrived there; early in the autumn of 1725, roughly a year
after Dyer's arrival, Thomas Edwards addressed a letter to George
Knapton "Al Segr. Jacomo Trevolla in Casa di Segnr Winder and
Aikman in Livorno. Via Franciae." And on May 21, 1726, Edwards wrote to Wray at the same address. (Ms. Bodl. 1007, pp. 59,
70.) It was not uncommon for an Englishman or group of Englishmen to take an entire house in an Italian city and make it available
to friends and acquaintances for lodgings. Such an arrangement
reduced the already low cost of living and assured the Englishman
more nearly the type of accommodations he desired than would the
usual Italian inn or lodging house. If Winder and Aikman had
their establishment running in 1724, Dyer may well have spent a
few days there before going on to other cities. And if this Aikman
was William Aikman, the painter, Dyer may have known him in
London.

to Rome. Like many another traveler, he was homesick at the beginning, and in his first letter from Rome pleads with his brother Robert to write to him.[5] But this feeling soon gave way to his interest in the variety of scenes around him, and comments upon various objects of art and antiquity become, as we might expect, an important part in his letters.

The Pantheon seems to have been his favorite building and takes up much of his attention, even in his first letter from Rome,[6] although the Colosseum and the baths of Caracalla were high in his esteem.[7] Among the sculptures, he mentions at this time the Hercules, the Apollo, the "Venus of Medicis," and the Laocoon, and among the bas reliefs, Trajan's column, the temple of Pallas, the arches of Titus and Constantine, and above all others, an ancient Grecian one generally known as the Borghese Dancers.[8] Of this last Dyer had purchased a reproduction, and could think only with regret of having to leave it behind when he left Rome, because he could not afford to transport it home. And he mentions many other objects of interest in *The Ruins of Rome*.

These he seems to have been busily sketching, for he wrote to a friend in England:

I can't get any views of Tivoli, or any places in Italy. I have been to inquire at all the shops. Those of Sylvester we have in England, and I believe poor plates, too; but I design to draw some myself, which shall be at your service. I am now about the ruins which are in Rome, and have drawn a great many, yet, notwithstanding these studious entertainments, I can't always support myself, and I frequently sink into melancholy for want of society.[9]

---

[5] Willmott, p. viii; *The Patrician*, IV (1847), 266. This letter refers to the earlier letter, which is now lost. The text occasionally varies between Willmott and the articles in *The Patrician;* I shall refer to Willmott first, as being more generally available, except when I consider the text in *The Patrician* to be better (*i.e.,* less broken up, or more complete).

[6] *The Patrician*, IV (1847), 266; Willmott, p. 30.

[7] Willmott, p. 29.

[8] *The Patrician*, IV (1847), 267; Willmott, p. vii.

[9] *The Patrician*, IV (1847), 267.

Dyer probably meant by the phrase "support myself," "maintain my spirits." But in fact, if not in intent, there was a double meaning here, and the phrase may be read to mean "provide myself with the necessaries of life." Artists in Rome frequently earned their living by selling sketches of the ruins and notable *objets d'art* to tourists, who bought them as tourists today buy postcards.[10] The first part of the letter I have just quoted suggests that Dyer was using this method also to augment his income.

The relationship thus set up between himself and other Englishmen may have cut him off from much English society in a way that would make him "sink into melancholy." From the very first he had thought the Italian people were "very reserved and deceitful." [11] And a tendency to be serious-minded himself may have limited his society somewhat also, as he suggests in a letter describing an evening's entertainment.[12] So that Dyer's sacrifices for the sake of studying abroad did not end with an unpleasant sea voyage but continued while he was in Italy.

Rome offered many compensations, however. Dyer goes on to say, in the letter from which I have just quoted, that it took only a morning on the Capitol or the Aventine to cure all his discouragement, his melancholy, his desire to give up and go back to England. And the seven hills inspired more than his painting. On another occasion he wrote:

I am not a little warmed, and I have a great deal of poetry in my head when I scramble among the hills of ruins, or as I pass through the arches along the Sacred Way. There is a certain charm that follows the sweep of time, and I can't help thinking the triumphal arches more beautiful now than ever they were.[13]

Willmott printed four short pieces, in addition to the longer work "Written at Ocriculum," which Dyer wrote in Italy; at

---

[10] F. J. B. Watson, "Thomas Patch," *The Twenty-Eighth Volume of the Walpole Society* (Oxford, 1940), p. 22.

[11] Willmott, p. ix; *The Patrician*, IV (1847), 266.

[12] Willmott, p. viii.

[13] Willmott, p. vii; *The Patrician*, IV (1847), 266.

least two of them were composed in Rome. One of them, "To Clio, from Rome," seems to have been a metrical exercise as well as a verse epistle, for Dyer made two versions of it, one with exactly one syllable less in each line than the other.[14] He was doubtless also jotting down fragments of verse which later were incorporated into *The Ruins of Rome,* and in his more nostalgic moments he may have worked on the third version of *Grongar Hill.*

The thing which, artistically, disappointed Dyer the most in Italy was the natural scenery. The antiquities had more than answered his expectations, but after Grongar Hill and the Towy Valley, the mountains of Italy seemed naked, and the rivers small or muddy or both. He wrote, "I am disappointed in what looked so charming in the songs of the poets, the face of the country." [15] And this same attitude is reflected in the opening lines of *The Ruins of Rome.*

Another thing which impressed Dyer unfavorably was the religion of the country. Dyer had the average eighteenth-century Englishman's dislike of Popery, and a number of his letters and poems deal with what seemed to him to be the lack of reason in much of the ritual and ceremony which he saw. Unlike many of his compatriots, however, Dyer considered his own spiritual state while observing that of others—in fact, what he saw, I think, made him pause to do some soul-searching of his own. The result of this may be seen, for example, in the fact that his lines "Written at St. Peter's," although definitely critical of the Catholic Church, are much more fair than would have been written by most non-Catholic writers of the 1720's.[16]

Dyer probably lived in or near the "English quarter," the Piazza d'Espagna and the streets nearby. Here it was possible for an Englishman to live much as he would in London. Dyer probably gave up having a servant and a few other luxuries which some Englishmen felt were necessary, but was able to call at the

---

[14] Willmott, pp. 15-16.
[15] Willmott, p. 25.
[16] Willmott, p. 17.

English coffee-house fairly regularly, and was able to get himself invited to the concerts, balls, executions, and other spectacles which seem to have been the main forms of diversion in Rome. He mentions the good music in one letter,[17] and no doubt had as much of the other entertainments as he chose.

It is unfortunate that we do not know more about Dyer's friends and acquaintances in Rome, particularly among the artists, and with whom, if anybody, he studied formally. The only authentic portrait of Dyer now in existence was painted while he was in Italy; it is unsigned, but it seems a good guess that it was done by one of Dyer's artist friends in Rome. Longstaffe felt that it was most un-English; he says, "The field is very dark, and the dress almost as dark, and the attention of the spectator is directed to the face alone. There is no good engraving of this picture." [18] I have attempted to remedy this lack with the frontispiece, but the darkness of the picture makes it difficult to reproduce.

While his main headquarters were still in Rome, Dyer made several trips out to interesting places in southern Italy. As we have seen, he was acquainted with Tivoli (ancient Tibur), and he doubtless knew the other old towns within easy reach of Rome also; indeed, his health is said to have been seriously injured by the air of the Campagna,[19] indicating that he made explorations even there. And at a greater distance Dyer visited Naples, with all the interesting antiquities adjacent to it. On one of his side trips out from Naples occurred what was probably the most exciting event of Dyer's stay in Italy; it is recorded in his "Journal of Escapes": "1725. Narrow escape at Baiae, from some banditti who harboured in the ruins there." [20]

---

[17] *The Patrician*, IV (1847), 268.

[18] *Montgomeryshire Collections*, XI (1878), 398. The portrait given with Johnson's *Poets* and all editions of Dyer's works which carried a portrait before Willmott's edition, was of Samuel Dyer, a member of Johnson's Literary Club and no connection of John Dyer's.

[19] Willmott, p. xiii.

[20] *The Patrician*, IV (1847), 265; cf. Willmott, p. vi.

The usual procedure among English travelers in Italy was to remain in Rome through Holy Week and then leave for Venice, planning to be there for Ascension Day forty days later. Some of the pageantries which Dyer describes in his letters certainly sound like those of Easter time, so that he may have followed this practice also. Easter was early, on March 28, in 1725, thus putting Ascension Day on May 7. If he followed this course, Dyer then presumably went on after May 7 and visited some of the more important cities in northern Italy, making, as his first biographer implies,[21] an extended stay in Florence. He then returned to Rome for at least a short time.[22]

Because of the very limited choice of roads available to Dyer, we can list a number of cities which he must have visited in this trip around Italy, but today we have memorials of only two of them. One is Ocriculum, the old ruins near the modern city of Otricoli, one of the first stops on the road from Rome to Venice. Dyer was unusual in being so impressed with these ruins; many travelers passed them by. But he stopped to sketch and paint, and here received the inspiration for his lines "Written at Ocriculum in Italy, 1725." The second is Florence, where he moved from the classical to the Renaissance period. Dyer must have found much to his liking at Florence; it is unfortunate that Longstaffe and Willmott did not see fit to reproduce any of the letters or notes that Dyer probably wrote about it. In addition to the "pittoresque prospects" which his first biographer mentions, Dyer enjoyed the museums and buildings in Florence itself; our evidence of this is one of his finest paintings, a copy of

---

[21] "Advertisement" in *Poems* by John Dyer (London, 1761), p. iii: "Besides the usual study of the remains of Antiquity, and the works of the great Masters, he frequently spent whole days in the country about Rome and Florence, sketching those pittoresque prospects with facility and spirit."

[22] In what appears to be one of his last letters from Italy he wrote: "I take the opportunity of a gentleman leaving *Rome* [italics mine] to write to my dear mother, and pleasure myself with telling her that I shall soon return . . ." Willmott, p. viii; *The Patrician,* IV (1847), 266.

Correggio's lovely "Madonna Adoring the Christ Child." The original painting was given by the Duke of Mantua to Cosimo II and placed in 1617 in the Uffizi Gallery,[23] where Dyer presumably copied it.

Because it is one of the most important of his poems biographically, we should consider here Dyer's lines "Written at Ocriculum" before we go on. His lines concern themselves very little with Ocriculum; they are, rather, a projection of Dyer's own introspective contemplations about his future into the mouth of a seer who appears to him in a vision while he is sketching at Ocriculum, "studious to excel, Of praise and fame ambitious." The figure warns Dyer against the vanity of ambition and desire for fame, pointing to the convenient ruins for evidence. But before this he asks Dyer to consider whether what he is doing is worth while in view of the frailty of his health; does he think that, even if immortal renown is to be had "in this fugacious scene," he will live long enough to achieve it? This passage (lines 22-35) seems autobiographical on Dyer's part and supports Willmott's statement that "his health, never vigorous, was greatly injured by the air of the Campagna." [24] There can be little doubt, I think, that Dyer had some serious illness while he was in Rome; he may even have been sick during his stay in Ocriculum. How much the Campagna had to do with his ailment is more questionable, for much superstition had grown up about the pestilential effects of the area.[25] Perhaps Longstaffe was more nearly correct when, in writing of a later illness, he said, "Indeed, for the rest of his life he was a weak, poorly subject, perhaps, having injured himself by too intense study in his youth." [26] In any case, whether his illness was the malaria for which the Campagna was famous, or the first (so far as we

---

[23] Georges LaFenestre, *Florence* (*La Peinture en Europe* Series, Paris, n.d.), p. 48; Maud Cruttwell, *A Guide to the Paintings in the Florentine Galleries* (London, 1907), p. 107.

[24] Willmott, p. xiii.

[25] Mead, pp. 310-11.

[26] *The Patrician*, V (1848), 79.

"MADONNA ADORING THE CHRIST CHILD"

A copy of Correggio's masterpiece, made probably when Dyer was in Florence
in 1725, and now in the possession of Ronald Hylton Smith, Esq.

know) attack of his later pulmonary ailment, it was severe and made him think about his future.

The seer then proceeds to warn Dyer that the alternative to a life of ambition is not one of ease and riotous living; there is "another path obscure, Narrow, despised, frequented by the few." He says to Dyer:

> So be thou just, and wise, and fill thy life
> With deeds of good; not with vain-glorious arts
> Attempered to short pomp, th'erroneous praise
> Of men vain-seeking, but humane and meek,
> Content and cheerful, with religious care,
> (In due regard to thy contingent state)
> Weighing what best may be performed, and what forbore.

Taken literally, this passage, and indeed the whole poem, is a denial of painting as a profession; it is also an expression of the sentimentalism characteristic of the period.[27] And we must be careful not to confuse sentimentalism with sentimentality; these ideas were deeply and sincerely felt by Dyer. Shaken by his illness, moved by the extremes of religious pageantry which he describes in some of his letters from Rome,[28] he had been considering his religious beliefs. Although the resulting ideas, which we meet here for the first time, may be conventional, they are important to us as they keep recurring in Dyer's life for the next fifteen years, until Dyer entered the church and definitely gave up all thought of making a profession of one of the arts.

---

[27] See Hoxie Neale Fairchild, *Religious Trends in English Poetry*, vol. I, *1700-1740: Protestantism and the Cult of Sentiment* (New York, 1939), pp. 441-4, 484-7. It is to be regretted, I think, that Professor Fairchild, in dealing with Dyer, used the edition of Dyer's works which he lists in his bibliography (p. 580): *Poems*, ed. Edward Thomas (London, 1903), which contains only six poems. Willmott's edition is unfortunately rather scarce, but it would have provided Professor Fairchild with some "divine poetry" by Dyer (the lack of which he regrets on p. 443) and much more material in general than does Thomas' edition.

[28] Willmott, pp. 16-7; *The Patrician*, IV (1847), 267.

The idea of giving up painting was still in his mind when he got back to Rome after his trip around Italy, probably some months after his stop at Ocriculum, for in the last letter which we have written from Italy he wrote to his mother, "I have gathered, I thank God, enough of knowledge in painting, to live well in the busiest part of the world, if I should happen to prefer it to retirement." [29] Apparently at the end of his stay in Italy he was having no trouble supporting himself with his brush and colors, unlike the beginning of his visit; he had secured the craftsmanship for which he had come, and from that point of view his journey had been highly successful.

Dyer returned to England probably in the late summer or autumn of 1725, having been gone about a year or fifteen months. We see Dyer's strength of will once again in his determination to make this tour at the time when it would do him the most good, regardless of difficulties. Many of the benefits of the trip are too intangible to discuss here, but it is clear that it affected the rest of his life in three imporant ways: it gave him an adequate means of livelihood; it precipitated or at least intensified an illness which was incurable; and it stirred up some very serious religious thought in him.[30]

---

[29] *The Patrician,* IV (1847), 266; Willmott, p. viii.

[30] Some notice should be taken here of the letter ascribed to Dyer, part of which was printed in the catalogue of the R. B. Adam Collection (III, 90), which collection is now in the possession of Mr. and Mrs. Donald F. Hyde of Somerville, N. J. Through the courtesy of Dr. Robert F. Metzdorf, formerly curator of the collection while it was on deposit in the library of the University of Rochester, I have a photostat of the letter. After comparing it with Dyer's notebooks which date from the 1720's and other examples of Dyer's handwriting, I am convinced that it is not in Dyer's hand; the signature is a scrawl which is hard to read, but which comes closer to being "J. Det" than anything else. *If* this letter is by Dyer, it means that Dyer made a second trip to Italy sometime after August, 1726, returning about the first of March, 1727. Unfortunately we know of no datable events in Dyer's life between those two dates which could prove such a trip impossible, but it seems highly improbable in view of Dyer's financial condition.

CHAPTER IV

"From Traveled Realms the Curious Swain Returns"

In his last letter from Rome Dyer had promised his mother that he would visit her in South Wales as soon as he returned from Italy; we may assume, I think, that he kept this promise. Dyer seems always to have been much more congenial with his mother than with his father and genuinely fond of her. How long John stayed at Grey House, her home after Robert Dyer, Jr. occupied Aberglasney, is uncertain, but it is unlikely that he would make so long a trip for only a few days.

Late in the autumn or early in the winter, then, Dyer returned to London. He came fully intending to set up in the metropolis as a professional painter. He had written his mother from Italy that he had gathered "enough of knowledge in painting, to live well in the busiest part of the world," [1] and his closest friends apparently agreed with his estimate. Even before he went to Italy, as we have seen, Clio, Savage, and Hill had praised his portrait of Clio; upon his return Benjamin Victor, in "A Session of the Painters," [2] suggested him as one of a number of possible successors to the position left vacant by the death of Kneller. [3] Dyer had apparently recovered from his illness and

---

[1] Willmott, p. viii.

[2] Victor, *Original Letters,* III, 17. Dyer and John Smybert are here introduced together in a manner which suggests that they were friends, although I know of no other evidence of their acquaintance. Smybert came to America with Bishop Berkeley in 1728 and stayed on after the failure of Berkeley's plan to establish a university, using Arthur Pond as his London agent. (See William T. Whitley, *Artists and Their Friends in England, 1700-1799,* 2 vols. [London, 1928], I, 62.)

[3] Oct. 19, 1723.

overcome the discouragement he had felt at Ocriculum and returned to his painting with spirit and enthusiasm.

A successful career in painting involved primarily portraiture at this time, but commissions were occasionally placed for landscapes and heroic subjects. Dyer had had experience with all three; Savage praises his landscapes and heroic pictures as well as his portraits.[4] In fact, Savage is so explicit in his references that one could easily believe that Dyer had painted heroic canvases of the battles of Pharsalia and Munda. Richardson felt that of all the various types of painting, the heroic was the greatest and the one through which any artist should seek to make his lasting reputation.[5]

The year 1726 probably marks the point during Dyer's residence in London when he was best known to the general public and consequently had the best opportunity to establish himself in his profession. During the spring and early summer of that year poems by and to him appeared in three different poetical miscellanies, thus keeping his name before the public eye. His own poems established him as a poet, of course, but the poems to him emphasized his abilities as a painter and must have provided good advertising for him.

The first of these miscellanies to appear was apparently the long-awaited collection edited by Richard Savage, which finally made its appearance in February, 1726.[6] It contained six poems

---

[4] Savage's *Miscellany,* p. 28.

[5] Richardson, *Essay on the Theory of Painting,* p. 40.

[6] The publication was not announced until September in Wilford's *Monthly Catalogue,* and the earliest review I have found is the notice of it in the *British Journal* for Sept. 24, 1726. But I have a letter from Edward Young to Lady Mary Wortley Montagu (to whom the *Miscellany* was dedicated), dated March 1, 1726, and saying that he has delivered to Mr. Savage her present of £20 (presumably her gift for the dedication). I think that what probably happened was that the subscribers' copies were released in February; before the rest could be put on sale Savage came to some agreement with Lord Tyrconnel, and the preliminary matter offensive to him and Mrs. Brett was deleted before the book was put

by Dyer, most notable of which were "The Country Walk" and *Grongar Hill* in its Pindaric ode form,[7] and five addressed to him, three of them treating him as a painter.[8] Only shortly after (if not actually before[9]) appeared *The New Miscellany,* containing an intermediate version of *Grongar Hill,* the first in octosyllabic couplets. This is, incidentally, the only one of the three to mention Dyer's poem, the most famous contribution to any of them, on the title page. In July Dyer's old friend David Lewis published the first volume of his collection, with two contributions by Dyer, the completed octosyllabic version of *Grongar Hill,* and a trifle addressed to one of the members of the Aaron Hill group, "To Aurelia." [10]

Meanwhile, he was associating with old friends and making new ones. It was about this time that the incident occurred to which he refers in "The Happy Disappointment":

> From traveled realms the curious swain returns,
> Sees a fair face, imagines charms, and burns;

---

on sale in September. Not all the copies were altered, and in 1728 Savage was able to advertise copies "with the original Dedication, Preface, etc." for sale. Cf. Clarence Tracy, *The Artificial Bastard* (Cambridge, Mass., 1953), pp. 76-8, 94-5.

[7] "The Enquiry" (44-5); "The Country Walk" (48-57); "Grongar Hill" (60-66); "An Epistle to a Famous Painter" (102-6); "To Aaron Hill, Esq. on his Poem called *Gideon*" (117-21); "To Mr. Savage" (291-3).

[8] "To Mr. John Dyer, a Painter," by Savage (26-30); "To the Author of the foregoing Verses [Dyer], a Painter," by Hill (58-9); "The Choice. To Mr. John Dyer," by Hill (165-8); "To Mr. John Dyer," by Clio (209-10); "The Picture. To Mr. Dyer," by Savage (294-8).

[9] Wilford's *Monthly Catalogue* for March, 1726 announces this book for the first time. See *MLN*, LVII (1942), p. 482, but cf. Edward A. Parker, "John Dyer," *London Times Literary Supplement*, XXXVIII (July 22, 1939), p. 437.

[10] Lewis' *Miscellany*, I (1726), 195-6, 223-31. The second volume did not appear until 1730. The publication of Volume I was announced in Wilford's *Monthly Catalogue* for July, 1726.

> Pure in his passion, tries each modest art,
> And every chaste embrace, to win her heart.[11]

But the poet was blest, the poem continues, in being repulsed; higher standards and Mira will prove kinder to him. The use of the name Mira rather definitely dates the poem as 1726, for Mrs. Sansom employed this *nom de plume* for a short time only, reverting by 1727 to Clio. Longstaffe says that in the margin of the manuscript of "The Happy Disappointment" Dyer had written the name "Miss Shen--e," a lady I am unable to identify further. It is clear, however, that Dyer was not insensitive to the attractions of the ladies; we have already mentioned Phyllis and Aurelia, and later he was to write three bits "To Celia." [12]

Through his friends in the Aaron Hill circle, Dyer probably met the man who was the most congenial of all his new friends, James Thomson. In his verses addressed to Thomson, Dyer emphasized their being frequently "at field in amicable parle." [13] One can quite justly, I think, visualize them walking and talking together in Lincoln's Inn Fields, or when time allowed, on longer expeditions to Hampstead Hill and other nearby points where they could get a taste of the country they both loved. The two probably did not meet until Thomson moved to London from Hammersmith shortly before his *Winter* was published in March, 1726, but by June, Thomson was inviting Dyer to contribute verses to the second edition of *Winter,* along with Mallet, Hill, and Clio. Dyer, however, "handsomely excused himself."[14]

---

[11] *The Patrician,* IV (1847), 425. The title is taken from Longstaffe's *Collations and Additions.*

[12] *The Patrician,* IV (1847), 425-6.

[13] Helen Sard Hughes, "John Dyer and the Countess of Hertford," *Mod. Phil.,* XXVII (1929-30), 318.

[14] Letter of Thomson to Mallet, June 13, 1726, in *Miscellanies of the Philobiblon Society,* IV (1858), 12; Thomson's *Works* (Aldine Edition, London, 1860) I.cxliv. Eight letters from Thomson to Mallet have been preserved, the originals being now in the library of Sir John Murray, K.C.V.O., to whom I am grateful for permission to see them. Fairly accurate printed copies are in the sources mentioned above.

By August, Mallet was writing to Thomson to secure Dyer's address in South Wales.[15]

During this first year after his return from Italy Dyer was also associating with the "set of gentlemen of both universities" who were helping David Lewis with his *Miscellany*. Of the identifiable men, most of them had been at Westminster either as students or ushers about the time that Dyer was there: Vincent Bourne, as a student, Samuel Wesley and Lewis himself as ushers. The main exception[16] was Wesley's younger brother John, later the founder of Methodism, and because of his later connections with Dyer, the most interesting of the group to us. Because Lewis specifies in his Preface that these gentlemen are "now in London," [17] it seems probable to me that the younger Wesley spent some of his time in London during this winter season, although nominally a student at Oxford, whence he sent his brother five contributions for the *Miscellany* on March 21 and April 4, 1726.[18] Here he met Dyer and established a friendship which resulted, eighteen years later, in his publishing two of Dyer's poems in a *Miscellany* of his own.

At the end of this first season of painting after his trip to Italy, Dyer had, as usual, gone down to Aberglasney for the summer, expecting no doubt to return in the autumn as soon as his prospective patrons had returned to London. But, as he expressed it to Thomson, "hard fate" intervened in the form of illness. Whether it was a recurrence of malaria contracted in the Campagna or another visitation of a pulmonary disorder, we cannot say. It was severe enough to keep him in South Wales

---

[15] Letter of Thomson to Mallet, August 2, 1726.

[16] Overlooking David Mallet, whose "William and Margaret" was clearly included for the sake of Bourne's Latin translation.

[17] Lewis' *Miscellany*, leaf A4 verso.

[18] *The Letters of the Rev. John Wesley, A.M.* edited by John Telford (London, 1931) I.26-31. Only two of the five poems submitted were printed: "To a Gentlemen whose Father was lately Dead" (Lewis' *Miscellany*, 232-4), and "Part of the xlvi.th Psalm Paraphrased" (*Ibid.,* 255-7).

for the winter of 1726-7 and yet not continuously serious enough
to deny him all activity.

During this enforced residence at Aberglasney Dyer either
renewed or made his acquaintance with Sir Richard Steele.
Steele had settled in 1726 at Tygwyn, in Llangunnor, just outside Carmarthen, and shortly after suffered a stroke of paralysis,
so that he was in failing health during this year in which Dyer
knew him most intimately. His interest in young people, however, was unimpaired. Benjamin Victor and the poet Robert
Dyer (a distant cousin of John Dyer[19]) both tell of Steele's de-
light in being carried out to watch the young folk dancing or
playing their games of a summer's evening,[20] and this interest
extended to John and Robert Dyer, two young men with artistic
aspirations. John did not leave any tribute to Steele as did Robert, but we may be sure that he found in the older man a sympa-
thetic and encouraging adviser in this year of adversity. John
served as witness to Steele's will on July 14, 1727.[21]

No amount of associating with Sir Richard Steele and other
interesting people, however, could compensate for the fact that
he was not in London pursuing his career. Dyer's notebooks for
this period are missing, but into a later notebook[22] he copied
three pages of prayers dated 1726 and four pages of meditations
dated 1727 which are all evidently from this time and give us
some indication of how depressed and discouraged he must have
been. The first few prayers all express a desire to be content
with his lot, whatever it may be; the meditations are generally
of a type intended to bolster his morale, but in the second one
we can see how great his depression was:

---

[19] He seems to have been related to John Dyer, at any rate, for
in his will, dated March, 1763, he left five guineas to John's niece,
Kitty Dyer, daughter of the poet's brother Thomas.

[20] Victor, *Original Letters,* I, 330; Robert Dyer, *An Epistle
humbly addressed to the Honourable Mrs. Elizabeth Trevor,* daughter of the late Sir Richard Steele (London, 1732).

[21] George A. Aitken, *The Life of Richard Steele* (Boston, 1889),
II, 320, 324.

[22] Notebook H.

I am far from grief, while I think I do my utmost, that in this life, though I am contemptible and pass away with my talents un-exerted—'tis soon to be forgotten and over and another state will succeed.

Dyer turned, as he had in Italy, to religion for comfort in his depression. Once again his thoughts reflect the sentimental-ism then beginning to be popular, but with the help of these prayers and meditations we are able to penetrate into his think-ing farther and see the man better. Religious sentimentalism is, to characterize it briefly, the religion of feeling or sentiment, and consists of a combination of anti-rationalism, a belief in the per-fectibility or at least improvability of man, and benevolism, all of which appear in Dyer's notebook. Sentimentalism is anti-rational in a variety of ways, the most fundamental being the belief that reason *alone* is not sufficient to control human be-havior, and that therefore aid must be sought from a supernatu-ral source (God). And not only is this divine assistance neces-sary, but it is clear that reason is given to man by God and is not a purely human power, as was asserted by the neo-Stoics and other complete rationalists. So Dyer gives thanks to God who "fillest me with memory and reason" and maintains the proper degree of humility by asking, "Shall the thing form'd say to Him who form'd it, What dost thou?"

Sentimentalism is still further anti-rational in its attitude toward the passions, which were considered evil by some people. The sentimentalists believed, to the contrary, that the passions could be directed to virtuous ends, and since they could not be extirpated, they should be guided. To do this, reason and re-ligion joined hands. This is the idea Dyer was expressing when he wrote:

We have a great disposition to be pleased in our younger years; the inclination overflows with kindness; the heart is then large; but the world soon contracts it in all those who regulate not their pas-sions, who know not the doctrines of philosophy, who are not ele-vated by religion.

And this sentence also expresses, I think, the feelings of a young man who has been through a bitter experience and is trying to learn from his experience.

All this led to the second main tenet of the sentimentalists, the belief that there was a natural tendency toward good in every man, that he was not utterly depraved. They saw that much of human behavior was controlled by emotion, and that this was natural. As Dyer says, "'Tis the nature of man to attempt the experience of that which he is enclin'd to, whatever persuasions he has to the contrary." But these passions, being natural, could be managed and guided, and so man could be improved.

Benevolism is the term applied to the sentimentalists' application of the Christian doctrine of good works. "Doing good" is one of the most elevating experiences a man can have and a fine example of how the passions control one's behavior; one performs an act of charity not because the reason tells one to but because of the pleasant emotional reaction one has. Dyer expresses the theory thus in his first meditation:

Our contemplations of God, our devotions to Him, the consciousness of doing good, and discoveries of truth are our purest and fullest pleasures; they die not in the enjoyment, fade not, but grow more exquisite and eternally heighten in the bosom of the possessor.

Professor Fairchild comments that the sentimentalism expressed in Dyer's poetry is characterized by a latitudinarian vagueness.[23] The strongest latitudinarian influence in Dyer's life had not appeared in 1727, but his thought, as recorded in his prayers and meditations, is vague in the sense that it is generalized. This quality is well illustrated by one of Dyer's most interesting meditations concerning himself:

---

[23] Fairchild, *Religious Trends,* I.444. Those desiring a more detailed discussion of sentimentalism may consult Prof. Fairchild's book, especially I.205-62. Very useful also is the introduction by Prof. Rae Blanchard to Steele's *The Christian Hero* (Oxford, 1932), pp. ix-xxix.

The fear of want and the pride of emulation which nature sel-
dom is wholly free from has often made me endeavour to point my
mind to the little and laborious business of gain, but such is the
weakness or virtue of my soul that she loathes the concerns of a
short and narrow profit, and obstinately attempts the cultivation
of virtues that never fade. She requires a wider sphere to move in
—yet a wider—unbounded knowledge—unlimited action. She cares
not to rest. She pants to draw nearer to her Maker in the flight
of an endless ascent.[24]

This passage reveals, I think, a mind still slowly maturing, a
mind that has not yet fully and specifically developed its philosophy of life. Yet it shows on Dyer's part a shrewd insight
into the conflict in his own character, what I have called a conflict between the practical man of business and the dreamy romantic. Dyer noted also, "Knowledge is much to be priz'd, but
peace of mind more"; he never found peace of mind until he
resolved this conflict, and he never did that until his sentimentalism—his philosophy in general—became more specific, as it did.

These prayers and meditations were intended for no eyes but
his own, of course. During the spring or summer of 1727, he
wrote two other compositions touching on his illness and state
of mind which were intended for others, however: his verses
"To Mr. Thomson" and "As to Clio's Picture." The verses to
Thomson certainly were written in 1727; by autumn Dyer was
again in London, presumably associating with Thomson once
more, so that the reference to their long separation would be appropriate at no later date; and it would seem probable that, as
the only copy of the poem preserved is in a commonplace book of
Lady Hertford, Dyer sent the poem to Thomson while Thomson
was at Marlborough with Lady Hertford in the summer of
1727.[25] In these verses Dyer is, essentially, saying farewell for-

---

[24] Willmott, p. 28, n.2.

[25] Alnwick Ms. 116, pp. 114-5. Lady Hertford quotes the last
four lines of the poem in her "Meditations and Prayers for the
Time of Sickness written in the year 1728" (Alnwick Ms. 115, p.
39), and adapted one line for a poem of her own in 1733 (*Ibid.*,
p. 88). See *Mod. Phil.*, XXVII (1929-30), 319.

ever to Thomson and admitting that he expects never to see him again in this world. Either Dyer's illness or his depression was serious—possibly both.

The fragment "As to Clio's Picture" is more difficult to date, but the despondent tone suggests this time. After saying that if he could ever paint her, he could paint Clio now, he goes on to say,

> Painting, great goddess, mocks my vain desires,
> Her lofty art a lofty soul requires;
> Long studies too, and fortune at command,
> An eye unwearied, and a patient hand;
> And, if I cannot brook to be confined,
> What scenes of nature should instruct my mind;
> At home, abroad, in sunshine, and in storms,
> I should observe her in a thousand forms . . .

He next considers that he has little life left (which would suggest a date close to the lines to Thomson), and that he has received little appreciation for all his effort. Therefore,

> Were it not better seek the arms of ease,
> And sullen time with mirth and music please,
> Hold pleasant parle with Bacchus over wine?

Here the poem breaks off, but it is obvious that the discussion is about to become that of the lines "Written at Ocriculum"; it was perhaps because Dyer realized that he had nothing new to say on the subject that he never finished the poem.[26]

Even though he had no new philosophical ideas to put down, Dyer tells us much about himself. In his lowness of spirits he apparently felt that he had not done well in his first year as a professional painter, and this thought must have made him even more impatient at not being able to build upon what small beginnings he had made. And despite his soul's contempt for "the concerns of a short and narrow profit," he had to recognize the

---

[26] Willmott, pp. 21-2.

need of a "fortune at command" if he were to succeed. He was now probably on his own financially, no longer receiving from his family the allowance he must have had while studying. His brother still had not paid him his inheritance, and family dissension on this point may have been added to his other troubles.

By autumn, however, he was at last well enough to return to London. One of his main activities was acting as a solicitor for himself and his younger brothers in a suit in Chancery against Robert Dyer, Jr. for their inheritances. Thomas was now twenty-four and had apparently met with rebuffs, and Bennet was anticipating them when he reached that age in August, 1728.

Part of Robert Dyer's unwillingness to pay his younger brothers was inability. He was, in the first place, a poor manager[27] and never able to save up large sums from his own income, though it was sizable. And secondly, less than seven weeks after the death of his father, he had entered into a marriage agreement by which he had transferred all his property, including even those lands in Llanddarog and Llanvihangel Rhos Y Corn which the elder Dyer had left for the better paying of his debts and legacies, to trustees. Robert Dyer, Jr., therefore, no longer had the power to sell any of his real estate in order to raise money and in this fashion satisfy his brothers.

The lawsuit seems to have been precipitated when Robert Dyer, Jr. secured permission from his trustees to sell the Lordship and Priory of Kidwelly in order to pay off the mortgage on Aberglasney and in the autumn of 1726 entered into negotiations with Owen Brigstock. The three younger brothers suggested that another piece of property be sold to pay them, but

---

[27] For example, he had to borrow money from John in 1734 (notebook B). In the Proceedings of the King's Bench, Entry Book of Judgments, is a verdict against him for £93, apparently for mismanagement. (P.R.O., Index Room 9635, and Judgment Roll 355), and in notebook D (the early notebook) Dyer wrote, "Much domestic damage and misrule has saddened my return." What "return" this applies to is not clear.

either the trustees or Robert Dyer, Jr. or both were unwilling, and so the only recourse left to the Dyers was an appeal to the Court of Chancery.

The resulting lawsuit is John Dyer's main legal effort and shows that he had learned his father's profession well. He must have been responsible for the bill of complaint,[28] dated November 28, 1727, although it is not in his handwriting. It is a tremendous document, almost five by six feet in dimensions, and containing 172 lines of about 50 words each, or roughly 8500 words. Included in it are an itemized list of all the property bought from Watson-Wentworth in 1710 and an account of the sale of part of it in 1715, of the father's will, and of Robert Dyer the younger's marriage settlement and later dealings with Brigstock. A Mr. Powell represented the plaintiffs as counsel, but it was probably through John Dyer's able soliciting that all the answers to the bill of complaint were filed promptly, and all other necessary matters tended to in short order. The various legal documents to be used as evidence were gathered together, and witnesses to them were questioned as to their validity at the home of one Mary Evans, widow, in Carmarthen on July 3, 1728. Finally, with all the material before it, the court gave its decision on August 2, 1728, roughly eight months after John Dyer and his brothers had filed their bill of complaint—a remarkably short time in the eighteenth century.

The court ordered that one of its masters, a Mr. Elde, should investigate the sale of the Lordship and Priory of Kidwelly to Owen Brigstock, to make sure that Robert Dyer, Jr. received a fair price. Brigstock later had some trouble collecting rent from one of his new tenants, and in the records of this lawsuit we learn that the sale *was* repeated in April, 1729, with John, Thomas, and Bennet Dyer taking part in the transaction.[29] Further, Mr. Elde was to determine what properties should be sold

---

[28] P.R.O., C.11.1260/6. For a more detailed account of this case, see my article, "The Dyer Family of Aberglasney," *The Carmarthen Antiquary*, I (1941), 30-42.

[29] P.R.O., C.11.1022/6.

to satisfy the claims of the younger Dyers. In December, 1728, he reported that he had found Mrs. Grace Lloyd, Mr. John Herbert (later the father-in-law of two of the sons of Robert Dyer, Jr.), and Mr. Thomas Phillips the most satisfactory purchasers of three pieces of property to be sold. When these transactions had been completed in March, 1729, it was found that the proceeds had not been enough, and so in June, 1729, a fourth parcel was ordered to be sold to Mr. Herbert. The deed transferring the two properties to John Herbert is now in the National Library of Wales[30] and is interesting as being signed by John Dyer "of the parish of St. Paul, Covent Garden, co. Middlesex."

Meanwhile, during the winter season of 1727-8 Dyer was at work in London, no doubt trying to make up for lost time with his painting. He was also seeing some of his old friends. One of these friends, however, dropped out at this time apparently. Clio's husband seems to have grown jealous of the Platonic attentions and Arcadian verses addressed to her by Dyer (and probably others in the Hill group), and asked her to break off relations. At least some such interpretation is the explanation, I think, of this fragment of a draft letter from Dyer to Clio:

The subject is too delicate. Had custom made us all free to unrestrained love, had law exacted no vows, I could then disturb the confidence of no man; I could then see and hear my Charmer, without doing an injury, real or imaginary. O Clio, I have often sate down with desire to do universal good, in the purest love, to be true to all. I have put myself in the place of the injured, and grieved at many things. For the future I am bent to do nothing that, were it known to all the world, would be thought unjust to any one. O Clio, forgive me, and still believe your faithful, &c.[31]

---

[30] Coleman Deed, D.D.256. See The National Library of Wales, *Calendar of Deeds and Documents,* vol. I, The Coleman Deeds (Aberystwyth, 1921), p. 67; *Archaeologia Cambrensis,* series VII, II (1922), 161.

[31] *The Patrician,* IV (1847), 422.

The letter is dated 1727; what the injury, "real or imaginary," was, we will never know, but the expression of a desire "to do universal good" is typical of Dyer's thinking at this time.

Late in the spring or early in the summer of 1728 he went down again to Aberglasney, probably in time to be at widow Evans' when the validity of the documents in the lawsuit was attested to. There is no evidence that he was or was not present on this occasion, and there was no need for him to be, but I myself feel that it is quite likely that he was, and that as a good solicitor he had been making sure all the necessary documents and persons were produced at that time. It is evidence of somebody's efficiency, at any rate, that they were, and that no one was forgotten and had to be called in later.

The rest of the summer Dyer was making a tour of western England and North Wales. In North Wales occurred another one of the episodes later recorded in his "Journal of Escapes." He was riding, and came to a narrow wooden bridge about fifty feet above some rocks and a great torrent of water. The noise frightened the horse halfway across, and as he could not turn around because of the narrowness of the bridge, he entangled his feet in the side rails. Fortunately Dyer was not thrown off the bridge, and escaped unharmed.[32] It may have been on this trip also that he learned of the episode which led him to write his verses "Occasioned by the Behavior of some of the Hereford Clergy, 1728":

> I hate the proud; the reptile of an hour,
> Whose little life is insolence, I spurn;
> I scorn him more (ridiculous vain thing!)
> Than the lone idiot, outcast of his kind,
> The naked mark of laughter! But alas,
> Alas, poor brother! why disdain I thee?
> Thine is no crime, yet be it—Pride alone
> Is that mean vice to be chastised with scorn.[33]

---

[32] *The Patrician,* IV (1847), 265.
[33] *The Patrician,* IV (1847), 425.

The journey was clearly designed to help Dyer observe nature "in a thousand forms," as he had said in "As to Clio's Picture" that he must. Possibly also he was doing more than just sketching; he may have been experimenting with living as an itinerant painter, a practice he took up in earnest two years later. If, as some of his biographers insinuate, he left London because he could not make a success of painting, he may have been led to try his hand elsewhere.

The fact that in May, 1729, he signed a document as John Dyer, "of the parish of St. Paul, Covent Garden, co. Middlesex," suggests that he was in London again during the "season" of 1728-9, although we know little of his activities. The Aaron Hill group of his friends, however, was breaking up. We have already seen how Clio had been withdrawn from his circle of friends. From 1728 on, Aaron Hill himself was too preoccupied with his York Buildings Company project and too much in Scotland to contribute much to the gallantry and poetry of the society. And Dyer seems to have drifted away from some of the others. Savage, for example, omits Dyer's name from the list of promising poets of the day in *The Wanderer* (1729),[34] whereas four or five years earlier he would never have made such an omission. At some time, however, Dyer did subscribe to Joseph Mitchell's collected poems, which were published in 1729 in two volumes, octavo.[35]

During the spring of 1729 he was again in South Wales, finishing up the details of his lawsuit and collecting his inheritance. Having finally received it, he invested two thirds of it in four South Sea bonds, each of which, he notes, had paid a total of £100 in interest through March 26, 1729.

He bought these on July 3, and five days later, when most people would have left London, he returned. He stayed for a while in unidentified lodgings in Covent Garden, then a popular

---

[34] *The Wanderer*, I. 325ff. Savage does mention Hill, Mallet, and Thomson.

[35] Joseph Mitchell, *Poems on Several Occasions*, 2 vols. (London, 1729). Dyer was content with a copy on ordinary paper.

area for Welshmen in London, and on November 18 took rooms with his old friend Arthur Pond,[36] who had a house in Great Queen's Street, near Lincoln's Inn Fields, and let the rooms he did not need.[37] Also staying at Pond's part of the winter of 1729-30 was Daniel Wray. Wray, although he was at Queens' College, Cambridge, most of the time from 1728 to 1741, kept lodgings with Pond all that time and was apparently there at least part of the time that Dyer was.[38] And probably Edwards, the Knaptons, and other habitués of Serle's Coffee House found their way to Pond's. I have no doubt that Dyer had been seeing these friends in other years, but this particular winter must mark the high point of his intimacy with them.

At the same time, he was associating with David Lewis and their friends at Westminster—although I think Willmott is wrong in dating Dyer's poem to Lewis, "An Epistle to a Friend in Town," as being originally written in 1729. The first stanza would be appropriate only after a prolonged absence from town, and must therefore date from 1727, while in the line "Then glide on my moments, *the few that I have*," the words which I have italicized express the spirit of the verses to Thomson and "As to Clio's Picture"—a pessimism which does not appear elsewhere in his poetry.

But in 1729-30 Dyer was engaged in an unusual amount of poetical activity. In 1728 he had begun a notebook for his poems;[39] he was, Willmott says, working on *The Ruins of Rome* in 1729;[40] and he revised the lines "Written at Ocriculum" in 1730. I think that the "Epistle to a Friend in Town" also underwent revision in 1729, having a stanza, first printed by Willmott,

---

[36] *The Patrician,* IV (1847), 423.

[37] We know the address from a letter of Thomas Edwards to Wilson Williams, Dec. 3, 1737, directing him to address him there. (Ms. Bodl. 1008, p. 197).

[38] Nichols' *Illustrations,* I.54.

[39] Notebook C.

[40] Willmott, p. 23.

added, and perhaps other changes made.[41] All this renewed literary activity was inspired, no doubt, by his associating with these friends of similar tastes. The revision of "An Epistle to a Friend in Town" may even have been carried on with some thought of its being included in the second volume of David Lewis' *Miscellany,* which was published in 1730.

Another friend about whom there is always a temptation to conjecture—her relations with Dyer are so ill-defined—is Lady Hertford. Among her papers[42] is a letter to her from Grace Cole, dated merely October 11, but tentatively assigned to the year 1729 by Professor Hughes.[43] Miss Cole writes:

> I long to be acquainted with Mr. Dyer, he has renew'd a verse that I have somewhere met with:
>> Fled from the Pulpit, from the Court, from Love,
>> Abandon'd Truth seeks Shelter in the Grove.
>> Cherish, ye Muses, the forsaken fair,
>> And take into your train the Wanderer.
> Perhaps it may be his.

The implication is that Lady Hertford had been writing to Grace Cole about Dyer; why should she be writing about him at this time? Had Dyer been in touch with her again recently? Had he visited at Marlborough on his travels in 1728, or on a special trip late in the summer or early in the autumn of 1729? The answer at present is missing.

On July 25, 1730, Dyer recorded in his notebook, he "left Mr. Pond's and London." A week later he arrived at Mapleton, his aunt's farm near Bromyard, in Herefordshire,[44] and a new era in his life had begun. As his curiously phrased note indicates, I think, he realized when he left that he was definitely turning

---

[41] The new stanza is preserved in his new poetry notebook—notebook C. Cf. Willmott, p. 114.

[42] Alnwick Ms. 22, fol. 157 verso (2nd numbering).

[43] Helen Sard Hughes, "John Dyer and the Countess of Hertford," *Mod. Phil.,* XXVII (1929-30), 320.

[44] *The Patrician,* IV (1847), 423.

his back on a career *in London* as a professional painter. He
continued to make painting his main activity for a number of
years after 1730 and accepted commissions and painted on the
side for the rest of his life. Why then did he leave London? A
number of reasons have been suggested: that he "could not
relish a town life"; that he could not "submit to the assiduity
required in his profession";[45] that his health gave out;[46] and,
finally, that he loved books, study, and retirement too much.[47]
The first of these is false. Dyer enjoyed and valued the intellectual life of a city, books, conversation, companionship, as
much in 1730 as he missed it in 1757 when he wrote to William
Duncombe regretting its absence in Lincolnshire.[48] But the other
three all contributed. As we shall soon see, Dyer entered upon
a piece of work with great enthusiasm, but when his interest
lagged he found it very difficult to bring himself to continue
with it. If this happened with a portrait or commissioned landscape, the person awaiting the picture might well feel that Dyer
was not equal to the "assiduity of the profession." And we have
already seen that Dyer himself had doubted whether painting
was the proper profession for him or not, although there is no
evidence that he was actually sick again in 1730. The income
from his inheritance was not considerable but was enough to
provide board, room, and some clothing, especially in the country. But most fundamental of all, I think, is the fact that Dyer,
even at the age of 30, had still not decided what he wanted to
do with his life. Not having found the immediate success he
desired in London, he withdrew to the country to think further
about his future.

---

[45] *Poems,* by John Dyer, LL.B. (London, 1761), p. iv.
[46] Willmott, pp. xii-xiii.
[47] Johnson's *Lives,* III, 344; Duncombe's *Letters,* III, 62n.
[48] Duncombe's *Letters,* III, 62-3.

CHAPTER V

"Pleasant Siluria, Land of Various Views"

In 1730, then, Dyer went to Herefordshire, and here he made his headquarters for most of the next six years. Two reasons seem to have dictated this choice of residence. One was that Dyer was fond of western England and Wales as subjects for his painting; he spent much of the first four of these six years as an itinerant painter in this area. Further, being the second surviving son in his family, he was to inherit his mother's share of the Cocks family's estates, most of which were in Herefordshire. And they were being badly managed, as we shall see, so that Dyer was led there also by the very practical consideration of watching over his future inheritance.

Longstaffe felt that if one studied the known paintings of Dyer so well that others by him could be identified, many of the paintings he executed on his tours might someday be discovered.[1] Some idea of the extent of Dyer's wanderings in this area may be gained, I think, from a study of the place names in *The Fleece*.[2] With points in between which are not referred to spe-

---

[1] *Montgomeryshire Collections,* XI, 401.

[2] He apparently knew the vale of Severn (I. 98, 716) and the Malvern Hills (I. 99) well, and he refers to Ross in Herefordshire, and the area in the Wye valley around there, several times (I. 50, 206; II. 37, 199). Hills or mountains, as we might expect, seemed especially to please him. The Wrekin in Shropshire, where he says he attended a shearing festival (I. 625-97), and the area along the Severn between the Wrekin and Dolvoryn Castle in Montgomeryshire (I. 698-720) were among his favorites. Plynlymmon (I. 193, 682), with the Vaga (i.e., the Wye) and other streams which rise on its sides (I. 685-6; II. 373; III. 434), Snowdon (I. 193), and Cader Idris (I. 194) also are mentioned.

cifically, they cover most of North Wales and "Siluria," that part
of England lying west of the Severn River. I have been able,
however, to trace in this part of the country only two paintings,[3]
both of the Last Supper, and both purchased from Dyer by Sir
John Pryce of Newtown, Montgomeryshire, Bart. Although Sir
John was known locally as the "eccentric baronet," [4] he was a
generous public benefactor. Between 1727 and 1732 he presented the church at Newtown with a set of communion plate
and a silver basin for christening and had the bells of the church
recast and three new ones added. In 1732 he presented one of
Dyer's pictures to the church as an altar piece,[5] and is said to
have given the other to the parish of Llanidloes, but it unfortunately has been lost.[6] The picture at Newtown is signed on the
back (as is the case with several of Dyer's paintings) and dated
1727, so that Sir John may have purchased it before 1732. It
seems likely, however, that the second, which is reported to have
been a copy of it, was done in 1732 at the request of Sir John
when Dyer was traveling along the upper reaches of the Severn.

During the winter months Dyer probably settled down in
some central point because of the bad weather and bad roads
and possibly because of the absence in London of some of his
potential customers. That he spent at least one winter in Here-

---

[3] As a possible sidelight on the successful vending of his wares,
it is interesting that the only private estates which he mentions are
3 in Herefordshire: Croft Castle (I. 52), the residence of his brother
Robert's brother-in-law, Sir Archer Croft, Bart.; Shobden (I. 55),
the seat of Lord Bateman, where Dyer may have visited his old
friend Lewis Crusius; and Eyewood (I. 53), belonging to the Earl
of Oxford.

[4] Rev. Canon J. E. Morgan, "Romance and Mystery of a 'Silver
Bason'", *Western Mail and South Wales News,* no. 21,266 (Aug.
27, 1937), 13.

[5] I am indebted to the Rev. Canon J. E. Morgan, formerly
rector of Newtown, for showing me Dyer's painting and some of
Sir John's other gifts to the church at Newtown. They were all
recorded in the churwardens' books at the time they were given.

[6] *Montgomeryshire Collections,* XI, 401.

ford is suggested by a letter, dated merely 1732, in which Benjamin Victor wrote to his friend Captain Apperley of the Marines:[7] "I envy you nothing in Hereford but the company of Mr. Dyer, whom I know to be a gentleman of great accomplishments."[8] He no doubt continued to paint during these months, but he also found time, I think, for the reading which was becoming increasingly important to him. The only poetry from these first four years in Herefordshire which has survived is an unimportant piece of eighteen lines of blank verse dated 1731 by Longstaffe. Called "Solomon's Choice,"[9] it is based on I Kings iii. 5-13, the story of Solomon's choosing wisdom over wealth and honor.

During these years of itinerant painting Dyer was also watching his future inheritance. His mother was co-heiress, with her two sisters, of the estate of their father, John Cocks of Hinlip, near Worcester, Gent. Of the other daughters, Elizabeth never married. Frances married first a Mr. Ivy and secondly, in 1733, a Mr. Williams of Brynhavod in Llangathen,[10] at which time she went to South Wales to live. By her first marriage she had one son, Bennet Ivy, who was expected to share the maiden aunt's estate with John Dyer. But about 1734 Bennet Ivy died, leaving John to inherit all the Cocks estates.[11] These consisted of the farm called lower Nicholson, in Hatfield, Herefordshire; Mapleton, in the township of Norton and parish of Bromyard,

---

[7] I am unable to identify this gentleman further unless he is the John Apperley who collected rents for Robert Dyer, Sr. in 1715 (P.R.O., C.11.1310/91).

[8] Victor, *Original Letters*, I, 9. A footnote identifies the Mr. Dyer as the author of *Grongar Hill* and *The Fleece*.

[9] Longstaffe's *Collations & Additions*. Willmott omitted it from his edition.

[10] Dyer's paternal grandmother had been a Miss Williams of Brynhavod.

[11] These details about the Cocks family come from Longstaffe's ms. "Some Notice of the Fore-elders of the Rev. John Dyer." I have found much helpful material also in Walter C. Metcalfe (ed.), *The Visitation of the County of Worcester*, 1682-3 (Exeter, 1883), pp. 34-5.

Herefordshire; and undetermined property in the neighborhood
of Droitwich, Worcestershire.[12] Mapleton seems to have been
the share of the maiden aunt, who was thoroughly unbusiness-
like and continually getting into financial difficulties. Dyer helped
her out occasionally, but changes in the family threw more and
more responsibility for her welfare on him as time went on.

An example of the kind of assistance he rendered her is provided by the records of the King's Bench. Although they are
not as satisfactory as those of Chancery in identifying by geographical descriptions (such as "of Aberglasney" or the equiva-
lent) the persons involved, it seems most probable that this case
concerns John Dyer the poet. On March 3, 1731/2, John Dyer
and Charles Rogers (presumably Dyer's assistant at Mapleton)[13]
met one Job Gardner at Tetbury in Gloucestershire, about sixty
miles from Mapleton. There Dyer and Rogers agreed to sell to
Gardner two lots of hops, totaling sixty hundredweight, for
£97/10/-, of which Gardner paid £52/8/6 in advance. The
hops were to be delivered as soon as Dyer and Rogers had secured some sort of writ issuing from the Court of the Exchequer
(perhaps a receipt for the payment of the excise tax on these
hops). So far the records sound very characteristic of what we
might expect Dyer to be doing for his aunt—traveling some distance to sell her hops for her. The rest of the story, however,
is not so characteristic of Dyer's usual business dealings, for he
failed to meet his obligations. On the 20th of March Gardner

---

[12] Longstaffe mentions a place called Comins, near Droitwich,
where he thought the Cocks family had long resided. The Visitation of Worcester for 1682, however, indicates that John Cocks and
his father Henry dwelt at Hinlip. If so, this estate must have been
leased, for John Burke in *A Visitation of the Seats and Arms of the
Noblemen and Gentlemen of Great Britain,* 2nd series (London,
1855), II, 81-2, says that Hinlip passed directly from the Abingdon
family who owned it in the time of Elizabeth to the Compton family whose descendants still owned it in 1850. There is no mention
of either Comins or Hinlip in Dyer's surviving papers.

[13] Dyer never mentions the first name of "old Rogers" in his
notebook; the younger Rogers was named Thomas.

requested Dyer and Rogers to deliver to him these two lots of
hops and offered to pay the residue of what he owed them.
When they failed to live up to their part of the bargain, he took
his grievance to court. What the difficulty was on Dyer's part,
and what the final outcome of the matter, are not mentioned in
the records of the case which I was able to find,[14] but the fact
that Gardner appealed to the King's Bench rather than to the
Court of Chancery suggests that Dyer and Rogers had experienced some trouble in securing the necessary writs from the
Court of the Exchequer.

This general supervision and assistance was not enough, however; affairs at Mapleton became steadily worse, and Dyer finally
decided to give up his itinerant painting and settle down to assume direct control of his aunt's affairs. And so, as he records
in his notebook,[15] he came to Mapleton on the 23rd of April,
1734. Taking charge of the farm and his aunt's business meant
no inconsiderable financial outlay for Dyer. On May 2 he paid
52 pounds for his aunt to Lady Williams of Castleditch.[16] Three
days later he "lent my Aunt to pay Mr. Haylings" [17] another
twenty pounds, and on the 10th five pounds to pay Mr. Davies
the maltster. In addition, Dyer notes, his aunt still owed him
£12/10/- of principal and interest from earlier borrowings. His
interest in Mapleton was rapidly becoming more than hereditary.

Mapleton itself was then what is called a "small holding"
of about 48 acres,[18] but the diversity of crops and the intensity
with which the soil was tilled meant that, as a neighbor, Mr.
Emmes, told Dyer, the normal staff for the farm was three men,

---

[14] P.R.O., K.B.122/143, fol. 490.

[15] Notebook B.

[16] Dyer's very distant cousin who had married Sir Nicholas
Williams, Bart. "Castleditch" is Eastnor Castle, near Leominster.

[17] Probably the Richard Haylings who was churchwarden in
Bromyard in 1732.

[18] For a more detailed description of Mapleton and account of
Dyer's activities there, see Edward A. Parker and Ralph M. Wil-
liams, "John Dyer, the Poet, as Farmer," *Agricultural History,*
XXII (July, 1948), 134-41.

two women, and a boy. Beginning with the week of May 6 Dyer kept a record of his workers and other accounts connected with Mapleton, and from this notebook we can watch his activities almost day by day for over five months in 1734—the only period in his life through which we can follow him so closely.

When he arrived, the buildings and implements were in a state of disrepair and the work around the farm was behind the season. The most conspicuous need was in the hopyards, where the plants, if they were allowed to grow too large without proper attention, would be ruined. Dyer, knowing little as yet about hopculture, called in a neighboring farmer, a Mr. Prichard, to supervise the work, and he, with the aid of Dyer's three regular men, "old" Rogers, his son Thomas Rogers, and More, and two extras, managed to put the hopyards into proper shape by May 20. The final plowing of land lying fallow, which should have occurred in May, had to be postponed somewhat while the iron plowshare of the plow was repaired (at a further expense to Dyer of 17s. 1d.). He did get "a couple of the plough fellows" who had a plow to come in for a day apparently, but most of this work had to wait, and consequently Thomas Rogers, who did all the plowing and heavy work around Mapleton, was still doing this plowing during the first week in June.

Other activities during May were more normal. The women, "goody" Rogers, the wife of the elder Rogers, and Anne Madox, wife of James Madox who occasionally helped out, were weeding the grain. The boy, whose name Dyer never records, seems not to have begun weeding until later. The men also found time to clean the orchard and repair the hedges of the hopyards and the commonfield. And Dyer himself sold two barren cows and a heifer, being reimbursed £10/5/- towards all his expenditures.

After a rather hectic month in May, June was quiet at Mapleton. Whit Monday, the 3rd, everybody went to Bromyard Fair —at least Dyer notes that nobody worked because of the Fair. And the main part of the work seems to have been the weeding, entrusted as usual to the women and boy. The boy, incidentally, must have been poorly clothed when he came to work for Dyer, for Dyer paid him this month with a shirt, a hat, a frock, and shoes. Old Rogers and More worked occasionally in the hop-yard, and Thomas Rogers finished plowing the fallow land, mended fences, and supplied what poles were wanting in the hopyard. In fact, in spite of having to pay "the fellows who got up the heifer from the brook" a shilling and six pence for their timely assistance at this little accident, Dyer apparently thought things were progressing smoothly enough to make it possible for him to be away, and so he left Mapleton on the 21st and did not return until the 29th. While he was gone the haying began, for which he had to buy new rakes, the old ones having been broken or mislaid apparently.

In July Dyer paid for the repairs, both carpentry and masonry, which had been done about the place, perhaps somewhat earlier. The weeds apparently flourished, for a third woman, Clark's wife, was frequently called in to help with the weeding. A high wind did some damage in the hopyard, causing extra work there. With the beginning of August came the harvesting and threshing of oats; Dyer's crop amounted to ten loads.

The busiest part of the season began on August 27 with the hop-plucking. In harvesting the hops the men cut the vines off close to the top of the hill, strip them from the poles, and carry them to some central point where the women and children pluck the pods from the vines and place them on a large piece of sackcloth, generally supported by a wooden frame or crib. When this cloth is full, the hops are taken away in it, either directly to the kiln to be dried, or to some clean and cool place where they may be kept until dry. As hops should never be plucked while wet, either from dew or rain, and as they must be plucked from the vine within an hour after being cut from the hill, all hands available have to be used in the harvest, that as much may be done in as short a space of time as possible.

Dyer had to buy a new crib cloth before the plucking began. Then with More drying hops every day, and the two Rogerses, James Madox, and "Hugh the Welsh fellow" working in the hopyard, and goody Rogers, Anne Madox, Clark's wife, Anne Newton and her seven-year-old daughter doing the plucking, the work was underway. Even with all these people, and four gypsies, "three men and a girl named Molly," who helped out the last few days, it took until September 18 to complete the harvest, although Dyer's hopyards covered only some three acres. On the 12th and 13th J. Davies the maltster and his son were present also, apparently helping Dyer brew his own beer.

The week after the hop-plucking was finished, another harvest began, the reaping and threshing of wheat. This part of the work was much less strenuous, and was done by the three members of the Rogers family and Anne Madox, and was over by October 8, when old Rogers was "thrashing the tail ends." With the harvesting of the wheat the busy season at Mapleton came to an end, and the rest of the autumn was spent in odd jobs and in putting everything in order for the winter—Thomas Rogers was cutting wood, and so on.

Dyer was no doubt influenced by the example of his neighbors at this time, so that it is probably significant for him and his later development that his first experience with farming came in a community where agricultural ideas were moderately progressive, as they were in Bromyard. The presence of a metal plow at Mapleton is a modern touch. Dyer's purchase of clover seed when the use of clover was still a sign of progressiveness is important, and he seems to have used the new four-field rotation of crops instead of the old three-field one. Our only regret must be that he did not mention his livestock, especially his sheep, more frequently in his notebook at this time.

Dyer seems to have been quite successful in his first season as manager of the farm at Mapleton, but his duties there were not all pleasant. On the 29th of May, scarcely five weeks after settling there, he wrote in his notebook, "I frequently wish I could abandon Mapleton with the fancied advantages of it— but the fear that by so doing my Aunt will be involv'd with troubles confines me." He later crossed this out, but it seems to have expressed his sentiments fairly accurately nonetheless. As we have seen, the first entries in his notebook after his arrival at Mapleton are records of loans made to his aunt, who was then in some financial difficulty. And his absence from Mapleton from the 21st to the 29th of June seems to have been on

business connected with his aunt and Mapleton.[19] On a leaf of
his notebook which started out to be a record of the men working for him in the week of June 16 are the very illegible and
rough drafts of two letters to his aunt written about this time.
A few of the more legible and coherent paragraphs from these
two letters will illustrate Dyer's attitude toward Mapleton and
his aunt still further:

What would you have me do (for I hear of great complaints)?
Would you have me injure myself while you say you are doing me
a kindness—you put things in a flattering light towards yourself and
others, and I fear by a false prudence you'll ever draw troubles
upon yourself.

Take if you please this my last proposal: instead of a consideration for the chance of the hopyard—I'll insist not on the reversion
of the 3 copyhold pieces this side of H. ford [Hereford?] brook, for
I own myself disgusted but will never oblige myself to live with
you at Mapleton—to have the house without reserve for myself and
let all things else stand as it was agreed on. If you comply with
this, I'll endeavor to give all I can to pay off your debts and make
you pass the rest of your life girdled with happiness.

The second letter was apparently written after his return to
Mapleton, and shows that he had seen his aunt and had been
negotiating to lease Mapleton:

I'm about to grant a lease of this farm for 21 years or for life.
If 'tis disagreeable to any scheme you have I won't do it but will
prefer any offer of yours which I shall think reasonable—be pleased
to let me know and I won't, and I'll wait a day or 2 for the favor
of an answer.

I have some reasons to determine spreading one way or tother.
I've 2 that would be tenants, and I've a purchaser or 2 beside yourself, yet I would feign give you a preferred— ? —for it at a proper
time, not to forget Mr. Bissel for both our sakes.

---

[19] Miss Cocks seems to have been living at this point with a
Mrs. Rea in Worcester—Dyer lent his aunt £20 to pay her on Oct.
30, 1734. Dyer seems to have been living near Mapleton, where he
was paying "40s. a year for the 2 rooms and 4s. per week, which
is above £10 a year for my board, in all £12/8."

I thought the last time I saw N. B. [Mr. Bissel?] of talking this matter over but I know not what checked me, unless it was that one rather blunders more in talking than in writing upon affairs one is not used to.

This last statement is perhaps over modest, as two random notes on this same page in his notebook show that he had not forgotten all he had learned in his father's office concerning the management of property. He planned that if he sold the farm, the bond for payment would separate from the deed, and he would economize on the taxes on legal documents by having his aunt make out the deed of surrender to some of the property directly, rather than transfer it to him first.

Just what the outcome of all this negotiating was is not clear, except that Dyer was in charge again at Mapleton in 1735. With a year of experience behind him, he felt it unnecessary to keep any notes apparently, and so his records for this year of farming are very skimpy. They consist mainly of entries of bonds signed, loans made, and taxes and tithes paid. In October, 1734, in addition to lending his aunt £20 to pay Mrs. Rea and a guinea to pay some unnamed person, Dyer signed a bond for £100 for his brother Bennet and two others, one for £100 and one for £50, for a Mrs. Price and her daughter, and made a memorandum "to get a copy of Aunt Williams's bond I gave for J. Davies." In the autumn of 1735 we find the greatest sign of Dyer's prosperity, however, when, on October 18, he lent £500 to Mr. Tomkyns, presumably the person of that name from whom he bought coals for drying his hops in 1734. And Dyer lent as much more in the following year.[20] This sudden

---

[20] The above transactions are in notebook B. The 2nd entry in notebook E reads:

		lent			
Tomkins	18th	October	1735	500
Reed	1	April	1736	300
Haylings	1	March	1735/6	100
Bradley	27	March	1735/6	100
T. Thomas	18	April	1736	50

affluence presents a slight biographical puzzle, as neither his earlier inheritance from his father nor his probable earnings from his painting seem large enough to account for it. The only explanation I can offer, and this is a conjecture, is that his mother died in 1735, and that in addition to property in Worcestershire[21] she left Dyer considerable ready cash, or goods that were easily convertible. This would explain not only his increase in wealth, but be an added reason for his change of residence to Worcester early in 1736. And, to continue conjecturing, the absence of notes about Mapleton for 1735, and the presence of such a poem as "The Cambro-Briton" in the "Mapleton" notebook, suggest that Dyer might even have gone to Aberglasney in 1735.

The renewed interest in poetry which Dyer showed in the late 1730's and which led to his publishing *The Ruins of Rome* in 1740 first appears in 1735. The soliloquy beginning "Too much my soul hath fastened on this world" is a Shakespearean imitation dated June, 1735 by Dyer himself when he copied it into notebook C, perhaps as much as twenty years later. Two other pieces, both fragments, are preserved at the end of notebook B, the Mapleton notebook, thus suggesting interest in them around 1735. "The Cambro-Briton" Willmott says is "From the MSS. of about 1735," referring probably to this notebook.[22] The fragment beginning "Man's happiness is peace of mind,"[23] however, Longstaffe says in his *Collations and Additions* is from a

---

[21] I am here assuming that lower Nicholson, in Hatfield, Herefordshire at this time belonged to Frances Cocks Ivy Williams because Dyer seems never to have referred to it in his surviving papers except in his will and apparently had little to do with it. Mrs. Williams was buried in Bromyard May 22, 1740 (Bromyard Parish Register).

[22] Willmott, p. 22.

[23] The fragment reads:

> Man's happiness is peace of mind;
> Who asks may have, who seeks may find.
> Nor more they ask, nor more they seek,
> The firmly faithful, wisely meek,
> While pure of envious hate and strife,
> They view thro' this the other Life.

manuscript of 1729, and in the Mapleton notebook he has written in the date 1729 over the poem in pencil. Apparently Dyer copied this poem over with the intention of reworking it and adding to it; the sixth and last line as it stands has corrections in it, and below the poem are notes indicating that Dyer intended to add at least two more lines.

These five and a half years in Herefordshire are not what one would call a critical period in Dyer's life, but during them he acquired much that he was to draw upon in later years. Most important of all, he was introduced to farming, which became extremely important to him, both as a means of support and as a subject matter for his poetry. He had acquired a financial independence which allowed him more leisure, and he seems to have been developing toward the end of this period a desire to write poetry again.

CHAPTER VI

"With Vigornia's Spires"

Early in 1736 Dyer moved to Worcester, and, as he says in a notebook (E) which he began at this time, he "took lodgings at Mr. Wilkinson's Monday, January 26, 1735/6—Agreed with the barber 31st January, paid to Monday, 8th of March." [1] There were several reasons which contributed to this decision to change residence. Worcester is only 14 miles from Bromyard, so that he probably felt that he could oversee the work at Mapleton adequately and yet be nearer his family's property in Worcestershire. Further, the first few pages of this new notebook which he began upon coming to Mr. Wilkinson's are filled with receipts for heartburn and various minor ailments which suggest that he had been suffering from some of them at Mapleton, and came to Worcester because of the better medical attention he could secure. Thirdly, Dyer's aunt was probably still living at Mrs. Rea's, and by being in Worcester he would be more available to her when she got into difficulty. But most important of all, Dyer was drawn to Worcester by his friends there and the opportunity they offered for the conversation and intellectual stimulation that were to play so large a part in the next few years of his life.

In Worcester Dyer knew or soon met a group of people with whom he enjoyed discussing literary matters. The most important members of this group were Dr. James Mackenzie and his wife, Dr. and Mrs. Greenwood, and a Miss Clayton. One of the first items in Dyer's new notebook is a prescription for heartburn

---

[1] Thomas Edwards, in a letter to Daniel Wray, March 14, 1736/7 (Ms. Bodl. 1008, p. 146) refers to Wilkinson as a surgeon and says that Dyer is still living with him. I interpret Dyer's note to mean that after five days he agreed to take regular lodgings with the barber surgeon Wilkinson.

from Dr. Mackenzie, so that he was one of the first of these with whom Dyer became acquainted, and it may be that it was through him that he met the others. And they, like the group at Serle's Coffee House in London, did more than stimulate Dyer for the moment; they became lifelong friends, for we find them almost twenty years later still receiving Dyer's poems by post and reading them with critical appreciation.[2]

The company of these new friends aroused Dyer to greater intellectual activity than he had shown for six years. He began the most systematic reading he had done since he was a student with Richardson, and to go with it, the most systematic note-taking. Notebooks E, F, G, and H were all begun in 1736 or 1737 and are among the most obvious manifestations of this revival. Another is his renewed interest in *The Ruins of Rome*. He had been working on this poem in 1729, but apparently dropped it before it got beyond the stage of being a collection of fragments. In 1736, however, he completed a first draft of the poem, and by early 1737 was writing to his old friends Thomas Edwards and Daniel Wray, apparently about the possibility of publishing it.[3]

His other poetry at this time reflects some of his other activities. He was still supervising at Mapleton during the active season, and from his experiences there comes one poem which can be dated 1736 fairly surely, "My Ox Duke." [4] After reading in his very prosaic accounts about "old" Rogers, "goody" Rogers, and Anne Madox who, as Madox' wife, frequently appears as "Mad wife," this picture of the same people two years later is interesting:

---

[2] See Dr. Mackenzie's letters to Dyer, 1754-7, in *The Patrician,* V (1848), 220-25.

[3] See Edwards' letter to Wray, March 14, 1736/7 (Ms. Bodl. 1008, p. 146).

[4] A prose account of the incident described in the poem occurs in notebook E, which was begun when Dyer went to Worcester. But Dyer was not at Mapleton much in 1737, so the likelihood is that the incident took place in 1736. I think the poem was written not long after.

'Twas on a summer noon, in Stainsford mead,
New mown and tedded, while the weary swains,
Louting beneath an oak, their toils relieved;
And some with wanton tale the nymphs beguiled;
And some with song; and some with kisses rude;
Their scythes hung o'er their heads; when my brown ox . . .

Dyer's compositions at this time or in 1737 show also that his interest in his friends in Worcester was not solely intellectual. Among the fragments of his verse are three brief poems to Celia,[5] who is identified in the margin of the manuscript of one of them as a Miss Fith— of Worcester. We are unable to identify her further, but that Dyer should be addressing verses to her so shortly before his marriage to Mrs. Hawkins supports his own judgment of himself, that he was fond of women.

Dyer stayed on at Mr. Wilkinson's until the late spring or summer of 1737, when he went on a trip to Aberglasney. We can date the trip by a dated reference in notebook G to a great oak (large trees always delighted Dyer; there are numerous references to them in his notebooks) on the estate of Sir C. Kennys at Keven [Cefn] Mabley, Glamorganshire, which he saw in 1737. And scattered through his notebooks are other jottings which may or may not be from this trip. The most tantalizing is a rough outline in notebook E of a mosaic pavement at Mr. Popham's, at Little Cutt, "near Marlborough." Did Dyer visit these antiquities on this trip in 1737? Did he stop at Marlborough and visit Lady Hertford? Do the two quotations from the *London Evening Post* during May, 1737[6] in notebook G

---

[5] Longstaffe published two of the poems in *The Patrician*, IV (1847), 425-6. The third, entitled "To Celia," reads:
> Pride from ruin guards,
> And love as oft with happiness rewards;
> But pride is folly; pomp and wealth are toys;
> Love, too, is folly; sense, and virtue, joys:
> Nice is the point, and e'er the man prevail
> Read, Celia, read his life's sincerer tale.
> —from Longstaffe's *Collations & Additions*

[6] They are the only quotations from newspapers in Dyer's extant notebooks, so that one is tempted to give them biographical signifi-

mean that he included London in his itinerary (even Marlborough seems out of the way on a direct trip from Worcester to Aberglasney or back)? A visit in London would explain the gap of a year in negotiations between Dyer and Edwards and Wray over *The Ruins of Rome,* but until further evidence appears, none of these questions can be answered.

When Dyer was in Llangathen one thing he did do was to visit the grave (in spirit at least) of his old boyhood sweetheart, Phyllis, who had apparently died since he had last visited Aberglasney. Among his papers were three quatrains on her death,[7] the mention of Celia in one of them dating them as of this period.

Dyer also obtained a few subscriptions for some projected work while he was in South Wales. In notebook E is a penciled list of names:

> Subscrip.
> Wales
> Dr. Claget, Bp. of St. Davids
> Mr. Brigstock   N. Williams
> Bevans   D--r
> Gwin
> Campbell
> Barlow
> Motherd
> Hill
> Jones

Some of these persons can be tentatively identified. Brigstock and Gwin are probably Owen Brigstock of Lechdoney and

---

cance. But they appear on a page with quotations from DuHalde's *History of China* (London, 1736) and Shaw's *Travels . . . to Several Parts of Barbary* (London, 1738), which he probably read later.

[7] *The Patrician,* IV (1847) 426. Here Longstaffe prints the three quatrains as one poem; in the *Collations and Additions* he copied them quite definitely as three separate poems. The original mss. are now missing.

Thomas Gwynne of Gwempa, two of the parties to the sale of the lordship and priory of Kidwelly to Brigstock, and consequently parties to the lawsuit of 1727. One would like to believe that the Mr. Hill was Aaron Hill, but why he should be included in a subscription list from Wales is puzzling—unless, of course, Dyer went to or from Wales by way of London and saw Hill on his journey. N. Williams is almost certainly Sir Nicholas Williams of Edwinsford, Bart. D--r probably refers to some member of the Dyer family.

Dyer fails to say, unfortunately, for which of his works he was taking these subscriptions. *The Ruins of Rome* would be a logical supposition were it not for the fact that there is no indication in the letters of Thomas Edwards[8] that Dyer and his friends ever considered publishing the poem by subscription, although they may well have. But Dyer may possibly have been seeking subscriptions for his prose work, "The Commercial Map of England," on which he began work in 1737, although this seems less likely.

"The Commercial Map" was another result of Dyer's new intellectual activity which should be mentioned here. As he described this work to Thomas Edwards,[9] it was designed to be a visual exposition of what natural resources and industries had been developed in England and where they ought to be developed further, with some antiquarian information thrown in. He intended to indicate on the map the products and exports of each area by tiny symbols—a little sheep for wool, a pole with a vine around it for hops, a tree for orchards, and so on. The map for Worcestershire, the only part of the map to sur-

---

[8] What we know of Dyer's negotiations with Edwards and Wray comes entirely from Edwards' letters (Mss. Bodl. 1008-9) ; the important passages have been printed in my article "The Publication of Dyer's *Ruins of Rome*," *Mod. Phil.*, XLIV (1946-7), 97-101. But if Dyer went to London in 1737 plans made there would not appear in the correspondence.

[9] Quoted in Edwards' letter to Wray, Dec. 7, 1738, Ms. Bodl. 1009, pp. 27-8 (*Mod. Phil.*, XLIV. 99-100).

vive, has none of these symbols,[10] but Dyer has written in in several places "coal," "mineral stones," "mineral signs," "brine springs," "salt works," and other notes of commercial interest. He intended also to mark all roads, navigable rivers and other waterways, and places to which they should be extended.

When he took up this work a second time, in 1749, Dyer wrote:

It is above twelve years since I drew up the scheme and wrote a discourse on the uses of a commercial map of England, and made some progress on the map itself; but finding it to be a work of much expense as well as labor, and meeting with no proper encouragement, I was obliged to lay it aside.[11]

The work was to have been dedicated "To the truly noble; and to the promoters of most great works, the merchants of England; and to all manufacturers, traders, and men of honest industry." Unfortunately all these noble persons failed him, and the work remained unpublished. But it had given focus to much of his reading. In the subject of trade, both domestic and foreign, his friends in Worcester had stirred up a new interest, a new topic for reading. "The Commercial Map" was the first, though abortive, product of an interest that ultimately produced *The Fleece*.

"Trade," he wrote in one of the meditations in notebook H, "is the daughter of Peace," and traders and merchants, he felt, were promoters of peace and therefore of civilization. And by aiding them to bring natural resources and industries together, to develop new resources, new manufactures, and new means of transportation, Dyer felt that he too was promoting peace

---

[10] This fact suggests that this is the part of the map completed in 1737, probably before the plan for the use of symbols was developed, although the symbols and dedication are both preserved on the sole surviving leaf of a notebook used in 1729.

[11] *The Patrician*, V (1848), 81. Longstaffe published only one paragraph of the discourse. The ms. is now in the Cathedral Library at Durham.

and civilization. He was beginning to make his desire to "do universal good" more definite and workable.

When he returned to Worcester, Dyer took lodgings with Mrs. Rea. After reading his very blunt statements about not living at Mapleton with his aunt, our only conclusion must be that Miss Cocks was no longer at Mrs. Rea's. She was probably in Monmouth, where, Longstaffe says,[12] she was living in 1739. And as Dyer's last entries in his notebooks about Mapleton seem to have been made in 1737, he probably made some final arrangement for the farm during this year, although just what it was we do not know.

Dyer was not through with farming, however; he apparently liked the life at Mapleton, and decided to become a farmer again, but at a place where the land was more fertile. Within a year or two of his disposing of Mapleton he bought two farms, Dowell's and Paget's, in the parish of Higham on the Hill, in northwestern Leicestershire. He had clearly been shopping around through the Midlands for some time with all the foresight he had gained from his experience in his father's office. In the Mapleton notebook, for example, is a list of questions to be asked the owner when planning to lease or purchase a farm:

> Queries
> Former tenant
> Present tenant—his circumstances and age when he entered and
>   for what time
> Old Rent
> Present Rent
> Repairs, and at whose expense
> Quality of the land
> General aspect of the country
> What timber, what manure, and the price
> Any lime, coal or other mines
> Materials for building how near
> Price of labor, carriage, provision

[12] W. H. Dyer Longstaffe, *Some Notice of the Fore-elders . . . of the Rev. John Dyer.*

How near a market town, distance from London
Sea, or navigable river
Roads, good or bad
King's tax, tythe—impropriate, vicarial, or modus, composition
    or in kind
Church rates, poors' rates, constables, highways
What methods used in tillage

On a nearby page he jotted down the names of several people
in Derby who may have been men to whom he was referred in
hunting for a new place: a Dr. Short; a Mr. Walker and Mr.
Waterhouse, attorneys; Thomas Gismal, a banker; and a Mr.
Erdly-Wilmot.[13] And he had probably done considerable traveling around in the area north and east of Worcester.

He was still living at Mrs. Rea's in March, 1737/8, when
Edwards and Wray sent him several pages of revisions for *The
Ruins of Rome*,[14] which he was still working on when "The
Commercial Map" and other activities allowed him to. But he
moved to Nuneaton sometime during 1738. He did not move
onto his farms in Higham on the Hill (a parish only two miles
from Nuneaton)—if, indeed, he had bought them yet—because
there was no suitable dwelling on them. Even though Dyer may
have thought about entering the church before moving to Nuneaton he still had not completely made up his mind. This fact
is quite clear in his purchase of these two farms. He may, of
course, have looked upon them as an investment (he kept them
the rest of his life), but at first he clearly intended to farm them
himself.

Longstaffe says that Dyer was living in Nuneaton when he
was married.[15] We have been unable to find a record of his

---

[13] This may have been John, later Sir John, Eardly-Wilmot,
then a young barrister from Osmaston, near Derby, who is mentioned in a number of the letters of Dyer's friend, Bishop Hough.
See John Eardley-Wilmot, *The Life of the Rev. John Hough, D.D.*
(London, 1812) pp. 231, 323.

[14] Ms. Bodl. 1008, pp. 225-9 (*Mod. Phil.*, XLIV. 97-9).

[15] *The Patrician*, V (1848), 75.

marriage, but it must have taken place in 1738. He married a young widow of 26 years, Sarah Ensor Hawkins.[16] Of her personality we can say nothing. Edwards and Mackenzie pay their respects to her in their letters, and Dyer himself tells Duncombe[17] that one of her grandmothers was a Shakespeare, descended from a brother of everybody's Shakespeare,[18] but history has preserved no record of what sort of person she was, shrew or otherwise. All we can say is that she came from an old Warwickshire family long settled at Wilnecote (about 12 miles from Nuneaton), and that at some unknown date she had married a Mr. Hawkins of Coleshill, Warwickshire (about 14 miles west of Nuneaton), but that he had died soon after, leaving no issue. Whether she was living at Coleshill or Wilnecote at the time of her marriage to John Dyer is not known, but in either case she was near to Nuneaton.

Dyer's life in Nuneaton can be sketched briefly from the few bits of evidence we do have. His intellectual activities held over from Worcester, especially at first. He continued his reading, his revising of *The Ruins of Rome,* and his work on "The Commercial Map." In November, 1738, he finally broke the news to Edwards and Wray that "The Commercial Map" had displaced *The Ruins of Rome* as his mind's first love. Edwards, in reporting this to Wray, was so aghast that he could merely quote Dyer's own words and then ask, "Is this possible?"[19]

---

[16] She was born June 12, 1712, and baptized four days later (Parish Register of Tamworth, Staffordshire, of which Wilnecote was then a part). Nichols (*LA,* VI. 83n.) suggested that George Ensor of Boston, Lincolnshire was Mrs. Dyer's father, but his will shows that he was her uncle.

[17] Duncombe's *Letters,* III, 60-61.

[18] Unfortunately no one has been able to discover the full name of either of Sarah Ensor's grandmothers, so no proof of her claim has been found, and most Shakespearean scholars look upon it with suspicion—for example, Mrs. Charlotte C. Stopes, *Shakespeare's Family* (London, 1901), p. 111. See also W. H. Dyer Longstaffe, "Ensor and Shakespeare," *The Herald and Genealogist,* II (1865), 295-303.

[19] Ms. Bodl. 1009, pp. 27-8 (*Mod. Phil.,* XLIV. 99-100).

The year 1739 brought distractions from bookish things, however. It was apparently Dyer's first full season at his new farms, and they took much of his attention. In addition to the usual farmer's routine, Dyer's burden was increased by the fact that neither of his farms seems to have had an adequate dwelling on it, and so he spent much of the time either repairing or building a house for himself and his family. Here he had another experience worthy of being recorded in his "Journal of Escapes": "Escape at Higham when the hole was made in a chamber of a pair of stairs, &c." [20]

A second distraction appeared in July when his first child was born, a son John baptized on July 26.[21] This child is another of the mysteries in the poet's life, for we do not know what became of him—yet Dyer named his second son John also, eleven years later. That the first son did not die at once is clear from an amusing and at the same time almost pathetic letter from Edwards to Wray on October 2:

You put a much harder task upon me in desiring me to write to Dyer. What can I say? I can give him no account of any proceeding about his publication, for it does not at present proceed. His planting and building, unless he had given us some account of it, will yield very little matter for correspondence, and for the cradle business, it is all *lettres closes* to me. I am afraid you are a wag and for these very reasons refer him to me.[22]

But after October 2 this John Dyer, Jr. disappears from the annals of history.

The publication to which Edwards refers was, of course, *The Ruins of Rome.* Dyer, in spite of distractions, had managed

---

[20] *The Patrician,* IV (1847), 265.

[21] Dyer is generally said to have had four children, all born in the 1740's or later, but his curious statement to Duncombe (Duncombe's *Letters,* III, 61), "we have four children *living*" (italics mine) made Dr. Parker suspect that there might have been another child; his suspicion was justified by his finding the entry of this child's baptism in the Nuneaton Parish Register.

[22] Ms. Bodl. 1009, p. 65.

to make the final revisions. Now the delay was being caused in London. Isaac Hawkins Browne, with whom Edwards and Wray were consulting, had hoped that through the influence of Lord Lyttelton they might get Dodsley to publish the poem,[23] but this project seems to have met with an early failure, we hear so little of it. By October 2 Edwards and Wray were unable to secure any publisher. Finally Dyer had to go to London to make his own arrangements. Some time between Edwards' letters of January 29 and February 12, 1740, Dyer came to terms with Lawton Gilliver, who printed the poem in a neat quarto and published it late in February or early in March.[24]

The poem was dedicated, on the recommendation of Edwards and Wray, to the Roman Club,[25] but the members apparently did not support the publication as well as they had hoped, and a second printing was not called for. It was published anonymously; why, is not clear, since they apparently hoped to capitalize on Dyer's having written *Grongar Hill* by including it in a second edition.[26] It soon became known, however, from the opening lines of the poem, that Dyer was the author of *The Ruins of Rome;* a correspondent of the *Gentleman's Magazine* in April wrote, "Mr. J. Dyer, so justly celebrated for his poem on Grongar Hill, has obliged the world with another, entitled *The Ruins of Rome* . . ." [27] This notice of the poem was very favorable, as was the only other one to appear at this time, in *The Champion,* the periodical published by Henry Fielding and James Ralph, for March 8.[28] In general,

---

[23] Edwards to Wray, Dec. 28, 1738, Ms. Bodl. 1009, p. 30 (*Mod. Phil.,* XLIV. 100).

[24] It was announced in the *GM,* X (March 1740), 152.

[25] Edwards to Wray, Nov. 28, 1738, Ms. Bodl. 1009, p. 20 (*Mod. Phil.,* XLIV. 99). The Roman Club was apparently an organization of those interested in classical antiquities.

[26] Edwards to Wray, Dec. 28, 1738, Ms. Bodl. 1009, p. 30 (*Mod. Phil.,* XLIV. 100).

[27] *GM,* X (April 1740), 196.

[28] *The Champion,* no. 49 (March 8, 1740), in the collected ed. (London, 1741) I, 340-7.

though, Dyer's work seems to have attracted little attention, and it was eight years before it was reprinted, in the first volume of Dodsley's *Miscellany*.[29]

Since he had been working on it in 1739, it seems probable that Dyer's new home was ready for him by the beginning of spring, 1740, and that about the time *The Ruins of Rome* was published or shortly thereafter, Dyer moved out to Higham on the Hill, where he lived the greater part of the next two years. The datable events of these years are few in number; during the winter of 1740-41 he returned to Worcester to paint the portrait of Bishop Hough and stayed at Dr. Mackenzie's in a visit protracted much beyond what either of them expected by Dyer's serious illness; on August 7, 1741 his second child, his daughter Elizabeth, was baptized at Higham;[30] on September 20 he was ordained deacon in a general ordination service in the prebendal church of Buckden, Huntingdonshire; on October 18 he was ordained priest in a special ordination service held in the chapel of the episcopal palace at Buckden;[31] and in the spring of 1742 he moved to Catthorpe to his first cure as a country parson. But these were two important years, for they were the climax of the spiritual struggle Dyer had been having intermittently for fifteen years. And thanks to his notebooks we today know more about his thoughts, as he turned himself in the direction he was to take in his pastoral work and in *The Fleece*, than we do about his physical activities.

This crisis was the culmination of several series of events in Dyer's life. The most important and the one I have been trying to emphasize was his difficulty in expressing his ideals in his life. When, in 1727, Dyer wrote in his "Epistle to a Friend in Town,"

> Fall in tune all adown the green steeps, ye cascades!
> Till hence rigid Virtue alarms me.

---

[29] Dodsley's *Collection of Poems by Several Hands* (London, 1748) I, 78-100.

[30] I am indebted to the Rev. Mr. P. H. Upham, formerly rector of Higham on the Hill for sending me a transcript of this entry in the parish register.

[31] L.A.O., Episcopal Register 38, pp. 403, 405.

Till Outrage arises, or Misery needs
The swift, the intrepid avenger;
Till sacred Religion, or Liberty bleeds—
Then mine be the deed, or the danger.

he was making the same mistake that Naaman made when he came to the prophet Elisha. It is unfair to Dyer, however, to take this as his final statement, as does Professor Fairchild;[32] by 1740 or 1741 Dyer had discovered that waiting for great moments and dreaming about heroic deeds will not cure that spiritual leprosy, frustration. He found that it was as necessary for the dreamer as the dream that he do something; the romantic dreamer and the practical man had to unite, to integrate, in some way. That they did I shall hope to show in this and the two remaining chapters.

Almost as important, and closely related, is Dyer's health. It is scarcely possible to overemphasize the importance in his life of his illness at Dr. Mackenzie's in 1741. So far as we know, Dyer had been free of any serious illness all through the 1730's, although heartburn and indigestion had caused him to worry. To be sick for a long time again now, therefore, even though he may have been suffering not from an old malaria but from a new disorder,[33] must have been extremely discouraging. A person whose potentialities are limited by health, as Dyer was beginning to believe his were, has to make adjustments; these adjustments were inevitably bound up with his expressing of his ideals. Dr. Johnson was correct when he said that "decline of health and love of study" [34] led Dyer to enter the church, but he was of necessity telling only part of the story.

---

[32] Hoxie Neale Fairchild, *Religious Trends in English Poetry*, vol. i: 1700-1740 (New York, 1939), pp. 442-3. Professor Fairchild, of course, had much less evidence to work with than I have had.

[33] Willmott's remark (p. xiii) that Dyer's health "was greatly injured by the air of the Campagna" applies most directly to the illnesses, possibly malarial, of the 1720's. Dyer's later sicknesses seem to have been consumptive.

[34] Johnson's *Lives*, III, 344.

Furthermore, a number of the meditations in notebook H suggest that he was not merely trying to find a way to do God's will for him here and now, but that he was trying to reconcile himself to something which had happened. The most plausible conjecture is the death of his son, a conjecture which is supported by such remarks as these in his notebook:

All men are not loud in their grief. The bosoms of some lock up their sorrows.

What hath despotic power indulged to live? The tyger, serpent, and the owl of night, all except man.

I strongly suspect that if the record of the son's death should be discovered, it will be found to have occurred in 1740 or 1741.

Fortunately two of Dyer's friends gave him good help at this juncture. The first of these was Dr. Mackenzie, at whose home Dyer was taken ill in 1741. Dyer was so grateful for the care given him by the Mackenzies that he addressed to them a little poem, "Written on Recovery from a Dangerous Illness," from which we learn that Mackenzie, in addition to attacking Dyer's physical ailments as best he could, also treated his spiritual needs through the modern method of occupational therapy:

> To pour around my bed the golden day
> Was noble art: 'twas nobler yet to light
> The internal lamp, and renovate the Muse!
> 　　How shall I thank him?
>
> Shall grateful poetry, with mellow note,
> And tuneful period, entertain his ear?
> Shall painting meet his eye, in nature's guise,
> 　　Sweetly delusive?
>
> Or, spreading o'er the poor my wide regard,
> Shall I attune the old Arcadian reed,
> And sing the Fleece and loom? That, that's the lay
> 　　Pleases Mackenzie.[35]

---

[35] Willmott, p. xv.

We know that later one of Dyer's paintings hung in Dr. Mackenzie's bedroom;[36] it may have been a present at this time. Unfortunately we have found so few examples of Dyer's painting that it is impossible to say whether his conversations with Mackenzie had much effect on his art, but it is clear, I think, that their talk did influence the course of his poetry. In his Mapleton notebook Dyer had written

> Give me to feed the poor, to soothe the sad,
> To lead a life benevolent and meek—
> This my religion.

Just how he was going to feed the poor, and just where his poetry was to play a part, he had not figured out by 1741. But his poem on his recovery shows that he and Mackenzie looked upon *The Fleece*, which is mentioned for the first time here, as an aid to the poor.

Dyer's conception of *The Fleece* was a large one, but one to which he remained loyal. And unlike the many other grandiose topics for poems scattered through his notebooks, most of which never progressed beyond the stage of a brief outline, this idea was brought to realization. He had to call on some of his friends for help at the end, but the fact that he had made enough progress for his friends to be able to help is due, I think, to two main reasons. One was that working on the poem satisfied his previously vague desire to "do universal good." In this poem he hoped to bring information to sheepgrowers that would help them raise more and better wool, and thus profit them; he hoped to improve the lot of the combers, dyers, and weavers of wool by pointing out possible improvements and extensions of their crafts; and in the climactic fourth book he thought of himself as aiding all Britain in trying to advocate an expansion of the woolen trade throughout the world. The second reason for his success was that the subject matter grew naturally out of his experiences at Mapleton and Higham on the Hill and out of his

---

[36] Mackenzie's letter to Dyer, Dec. 26, 1754; *The Patrician,* V (1848), 220.

reading for the previous six years; much of the thought expended on "The Commercial Map" was of use in *The Fleece*. And for the next ten years he was to be living with sheepraisers in Leicestershire and hearing much of their problems.

The second friend to help Dyer at this time was John Hough, the elderly Bishop of Worcester, whose portrait he was painting when he was taken ill. Bishop Hough was in his ninety-first year at the time, having had a distinguished career from the time of James II on. Dyer quotes twice in notebook H from his conversation with Hough during "sittings":

I have an aversion to religious controversy. Our treatment of those who differ from us is usually very unchristian. To treat men of all persuasions, all mankind, as our brothers, to love one another, this is Christianity if I know it.

> Hough, Bishop of Worcester, in conversation with Capt. Congreve and myself.[37]

And what is either the same idea from another occasion or another version of the same conversation:

To live soberly and love one another, to treat even the Jew as our brother, this is Christianity if I know it.

> Dr. H—Bishop of Worcester

Similar views appear also among Dyer's own meditations at this time:

I think (considering the many evil dispositions of men) that Virtue in any dress should be recommended, but many are of another mind; and there abound in all nations certain narrow formalists who are for preventing any application of good which is not made after their own manner.

---

[37] Capt. Congreve came from Stratton, Staffordshire, of the family of Congreve the dramatist. He is mentioned in Bishop Hough's letters, and was left ten guineas for mourning by the bishop's will. See John Eardley-Wilmot, *The Life of the Rev. John Hough, D.D.* (London, 1812), pp. 102, 164, 167.

BISHOP JOHN HOUGH (1650-1743)

Painted by Dyer in the winter of 1740-41. The original is now in Hartlebury Castle, the residence of the Bishops of Worcester. This reproduction is taken from the plate in John Eardley-Wilmot, *The Life of the Rev. John Hough, D.D.* (London, 1812).

A truly charitable man is towards his brethren a latitudinarian
—our Saviour himself was.

And Dyer, like his friend, was henceforth a latitudinarian. This
does not mean, however, that his theological views were hazy.

Just as important as the ideas directly traceable to him is the
reading which Bishop Hough probably inspired. Notebook H
today falls into several distinct sections, one of which is devoted
to works of theology, the majority of them being from the
"intellectual" school of Samuel Clarke and all likely to have been
suggested by a low churchman such as Bishop Hough. Here
we find Dyer reading Clarke's *Demonstration of the Being and
Attributes of God* (1704), William Wollaston's elaboration upon
Clarke's theories in *The Religion of Nature Delineated* (1722),
and Dean William Sherlock's *Sermons* (1707), while elsewhere
in the notebook he quotes from the work of another follower of
Clarke, John Balguy's *The Foundation of Moral Goodness*
(1728). Other works which he quotes in this main theological
section are David Derodon's *Funeral of the Mass* (1663) and
the very popular *Advice to a Friend* (1673) by Bishop Simon
Patrick, who had been a leader with Bishop Hough in the op-
position to James II. Sandwiched in (Dyer apparently liked to
keep two books going at the same time) are a number of extracts from *The Spectator*.

The ideas of Clarke and his followers rapidly became those
of Dyer. For example, he quotes from Clarke's *Demonstration*:

The Supreme Being, because he is infinite, must be everywhere
present, and because he is an infinite mind or intelligence, therefore wherever he is, his knowledge is, which is inseparable from his
being, and must therefore be infinite likewise; and wherever his
infinite knowledge is it must necessarily have a full and perfect
prospect of all things, and nothing can be concealed from its inspec-
tion; he includes and surrounds everything with his boundless presence and penetrates every part of their substance with his all-seeing
eye; so that the inmost nature and essence of all things are per-

fectly naked and open to his view; and even the deepest thoughts of intelligent beings themselves, manifest in his sight.[38]

In the section of his notebook devoted to his own meditations, Dyer condenses this into:

We ought to live in a constant sense of the Deity, that he is ever before us, and knows us to the depth of the heart in all our thoughts.

These ideas were a drastic change from the sentimentalism of Dyer's earlier years. Clarke was the leading exponent of the rationalistic school of thought that felt that the existence of God could be proved by reason alone—the very idea which Steele and other religious sentimentalists had opposed most keenly. This rationalist position comes close to deism,[39] but Clarke was also an outstanding controversialist against the deists and used his rationalism to prove such theistic points as the necessity of divine revelation. To many of his opponents and later critics this has seemed an inconsistency, but to Dyer, untrained in professional theology, these finer points did not appear, whereas the rationalism appealed with its certainty, the definiteness with which it offered something to believe in, and so Dyer accepted these doctrines without any feeling of being inconsistent or unorthodox.

Dyer also drew heavily upon Clarke's follower, William Wollaston, for inspiration. In *The Religion of Nature Delineated* Dyer seems to have been most impressed (as was Sir Leslie Stephen more than a century later[40]) with Wollaston's argument for the immortality of the soul. Dyer quotes three times from the ten-page passage in which Wollaston argues that there is so

---

[38] Samuel Clarke, *A Demonstration of the Being and Attributes of God* (7th edn., London, 1728), pp. 106-7 paraphrased.

[39] Deism in the common usage of the term—"the idea of God as an external creator who made the world, set it under certain laws, and then left it alone." (*CHEL,* IX, 292). This is essentially the same conception of deism as Clarke's in the *Demonstration* (quoted, *Ibid.,* 292 n.).

[40] Sir Leslie Stephen, *History of English Thought in the Eighteenth Century* (London 1876; 3rd ed. 1902), i. 131-4.

much evil in the world, there must be another world where "proper amends may be made." [41] Dyer's third quotation shows what ideas were appealing to him in this new theology:

How strong, how irresistible, is the argument for immortality in that man who endeavours in the conduct of his life to observe the laws of reason, who laments and labours against his own infirmities; implores the divine mercy; prays for some better state hereafter; acts and lives in the hopes of one; and denies himself many things upon that view; in him, who by the exaltation of his reason and upper faculties and that, which is certainly the effect of real and useful philosophy, the practice of virtue, is still approaching toward a higher manner of being, and doth already taste something spiritual and above this world. [42]

The inevitability of evil is a denial of the old sentimentalist theory of the perfectability of man—another noticeable change in Dyer's thinking.

And finally, reason has obviously replaced sentiment as the control of behavior. Benevolism, or "the practice of Virtue," arises not from the fine feeling the doer has, but from the grim, realistic picture (especially as Wollaston paints it) of the world, and the purely rational realization that things need to be rectified, to be made to conform to nature's pattern, or to "fit." Dyer practically outlined this "fitness" theory of morality of Clarke's on one page of his meditations:

Virtue or moral goodness is the conformity of our moral actions to the reasons of things.

Moral actions are such as are knowingly directed toward some object intelligent or sensible.

The conformity of such actions to Reason, or the rectitude of them, is their agreeableness to the natures and circumstances of the agents or objects.

---

[41] William Wollaston, *The Religion of Nature Delineated,* 6th ed. (London, 1738), p. 203.

[42] Wollaston, *Religion of Nature Delineated,* p. 210 paraphrased.

Relations between things or persons are their comparative states or modes of existence, necessarily arising from their different natures or circumstances.

The "harmony" which thus existed in the universe was much like that developed by the deists, but as Professor Fairchild says,[43] it is not necessary to label Dyer a deist because he accepted such a system; he could find it in perfectly orthodox, though latitudinarian, writers.

Dyer was still absorbing these new ideas, when he returned to Higham for the summer season of 1741. Here a third person who helped his recovery appeared, his daughter Elizabeth, who was baptized there on August 7. She seems always to have been Dyer's favorite child, and of all his children the most sensitive and the one most like him.

In the autumn he made his two visits to Buckden. On one of these he apparently visited Huntingdon itself, for he comments in notebook G on the view from Huntingdon Castle out over the largest meadow in England (physical size and sublimity were related for many eighteenth-century thinkers, including Dyer). It seems curious perhaps that he was not ordained by Bishop Hough, who had already done so much for him, but by Bishop Richard Reynolds of Lincoln. The fact, however, that Dyer's first parish after ordination was to be in this diocese, if he knew of it then, may have helped to draw him to Buckden; even more important would have been the fact that he had been associated with the parish of Fenny Drayton, which also was then in the diocese of Lincoln.

Dyer had probably been helping out at Fenny Drayton even before he was ordained, for the record of his ordination as deacon in the Episcopal Register reads "John Dyer, clerk, titled in the church of Fenny Drayton, Leicestershire." [44] The rector of Fenny Drayton at this time was John Ryder, whom Dyer had probably

---

[43] Fairchild, *Religious Trends,* I, 444.

[44] L.A.O., Epis. Reg. 38, p. 403.

met through Daniel Wray.[45] About the time that Dyer was ordained, however, Ryder (who was also Vicar of Nuneaton) left
to become Bishop of Killaloe in Ireland, and as the new incumbent, Philip Bracebridge, was not instituted to the Rectory of
Fenny Drayton until February 5, 1741/2,[46] Dyer was for several months in sole charge of the parish, with the title of curate,[47]
and here began to learn in earnest what it meant to enter the
church.

The winter of 1741-2, then, Dyer spent preparing for his
new position. This would include such mundane things as finding a tenant for his farms and getting ready to move. It would
also include much spiritual contemplation, and some of the reading which we have been discussing may well have been done as
late as at this time as he thought of the duties of the life to
which he had now finally and definitely committed himself.
Just when he moved to Catthorpe is not clear. For a while in
1742 he seems to have carried on his work in both his parishes;
for example, at the episcopal visitation in Leicester in August,
1742, Dyer made out, signed, and presented the Glebe Terriers
(listing the church property in a parish) for both Fenny Drayton
and Catthorpe.[48]

[45] Ryder and Wray had been at Queens' College, Cambridge,
together.

[46] L.A.O., Epis. Reg. 38, p. 408.

[47] The parish register transcripts for the year (o.s.) March 26,
1741, to March 25, 1742, are unsigned, but appear to be in the
same hand as Dyer's later, signed transcripts from Catthorpe. They
are now deposited in the Leicester Museum, and I am indebted to
the Keeper of Archives, Mr. G. Allen Chinnery, for this information.

[48] The clergy calls and other records of episcopal visitations
begin with the visitations of 1745, so the exact date of this visitation is missing. The Terrier for Catthorpe is dated August 23,
1742, and the one for Fenny Drayton, August 24, 1742, suggesting
that the visitation was not far off. Both documents are entirely in
Dyer's hand and are now in the L.A.O.; I am indebted to Mrs.
Joan Varley of the L.A.O. for sending me transcripts of each.

CHAPTER VII

"Tripontian Fields"

Dyer's first parish after his ordination was Catthorpe,[1] the southernmost and one of the smallest of the parishes of Leicestershire. Situated for the most part on ground rising gently from the Avon River, which separates it from Northamptonshire, it provided an ideal place for Dyer to begin his clerical career. The smallness of the parish (it was only about 625 acres in extent) meant that the pastoral work was light, and at first at least Dyer had more time for sermons and other things. The beauty of the country must have appealed to his artist's eye, and the famous Roman remains centering around Watling Street and Tripontium,[2] to his antiquarian interest. And the presence around him of sheep growers all the time, of course, kept alive his interest in *The Fleece*.

The church records of his parish give us a good insight into Dyer as he entered the church. The same orderly quality of mind that had been appealed to by a rationalistic philosophy made him an excellent administrator in his parishes, and everywhere he went the buildings and grounds were always kept in good condition. The registers most obviously show this quality. Instead of writing each entry across the page in chronological order as was the general custom then, he preferred to classify each marriage, baptism and burial under its proper heading, and to that end ruled each folio into three vertical columns. And at

---

[1] He was instituted "to the Rectory of Thorp Thomas, alias Colthrop, vacant by cession of Edward Wheeler, the last incumbent," on April 30, 1742 (L.A.O., Epis. Reg. 38, p. 413); he was inducted into the rectory May 2 (Parish Register).

[2] Watling Street separates Catthorpe from Warwickshire on the southwest; where it crosses the Avon (Dowbridge) is said to have been the site of the Roman fortress Tripontium.

Catthorpe, where the entries averaged less than five a year and were never more than seven, he went to the additional trouble of recording the dates of birth as well as baptism of the children.

Four entries in the register concern members of Dyer's own family. His daughter Sarah was born on July 13 and baptized on August 12, 1744, while a year later Catherine was born on August 2 and baptized the 11th of the same month. His second son, also named John, was born January 30, 1750/1, and baptized on February 16. There is no reference in the Catthorpe register to Dyer's first son, John, who probably died before his father moved there. And on September 7, 1745, a Mrs. Elizabeth Cocks was buried at Catthorpe. As this entry is the only one pertaining to a person with the surname Cocks in the Catthorpe register, it seems logical to suppose that this person was Dyer's aunt, and that she had been living with her nephew for a time before her death.

Even more revealing are the churchwardens' books, which begin in 1745, possibly as a result of some suggestion gained at the episcopal visitation which he attended at Leicester on August 12, 1745.[3] Some of the early entries are especially interesting as showing how parallel were his conceptions of *The Fleece* and of his duties as a clergyman. On March 31, 1746 occurs this record: "Paid for a paper to be read in Church about the distemper among the cattle, 2s." Two similar entries occur later in the same year, and there are eight in 1747,[4] when the distemper was at its worst in England.[5] Education was the first step in "the exaltation of the reason and upper faculties" to "taste something spiritual and above this world."[6] And in so

---

[3] L.A.O., *Libri Cleri* 18 A, fol. 14d and 18 B, fol. 144d.

[4] Christopher Holme, *A History of the Midland Counties* (Rugby, 1891), p. 138.

[5] In Jan. 1747 Dyer's old friend Dr. Mackenzie and the three other physicians of Worcester approved a cure of the distemper advanced by a Dr. Barker; see *GM*, XVII (1747), 18. No doubt one of the papers read at Catthorpe dealt with this cure.

[6] Wollaston, *Religion of Nature Delineated*, p. 210. See above, chapter VI, p. 111.

far as education helped his parishioners economically, Dyer felt he was carrying out Christ's injunction, "Feed my sheep," and that the work was therefore worthy of the church.

A third set of records which are helpful at least biographically are the records of the triennial episcopal visitations. There were four of his deanery (Guthlaxton) while Dyer was at Catthorpe: the first in August, 1742, just after he had begun his work and the one on August 12, 1745 at Leicester, we have already noticed; a third was at Market Harborough on July 23, 1748 when Dyer appeared and "exhibited";[7] and the last was at Leicester again on August 1, 1751, when Dyer was excused,[8] as we shall see. Willmott printed a paragraph from a visitation sermon,[9] but as Dyer could have preached this while at Coningsby, the selection may not be for any of these occasions. Dyer's sermons, of course, would be the most valuable documents of all in revealing his conception of his duties as a clergyman, his theology, and his philosophy of life, but they unfortunately have disappeared quite recently.

The clergy call for the 1745 visitation says that Dyer "lives near Rugby, Warwickshire," suggesting that Dyer did not live then, at least, in the rectory at Catthorpe.[10] Why he chose to

---

[7] L.A.O., *Libri Cleri* 19 A, fol. 3d and 19 B, fol. 5. "Exhibited" means that Dyer was required to show his papers of ordination, institution, and dispensations, if any.

[8] L.A.O., *Libri Cleri* 20 A, fol. 4d, and 20 C, fol. 12d.

[9] Willmott, p. xxx.

[10] L.A.O., *Liber Cleri* 18 A, fol. 14d. The fact that Dyer may actually have lived across Watling Street in Warwickshire may account for the story that his first cure was in that county. The legend was advanced by Dyer's first biographer (*Poems*, 1761, p. iv.) and perpetuated by Willmott (p. xiv). Neither of them names a parish, but Dyer's last descendant through his daughter Catherine, his great-granddaughter Catherine Dyer Hewitt, wrote to Longstaffe that the poet began his clerical duties as curate of the church at Stratford-on-Avon (from a letter now belonging to Longstaffe's grandson, Mr. R. H. Smith of Cottingham). The registers at Stratford show no evidence that Dyer was ever there in an official capacity, however, and the records of the diocese of Worcester give no trace of any official connection with any parish in Warwickshire.

live out of the rectory it is hard to say. One suggestion is that
it was in order to be nearer his glebe land—his stipend was £80
a year and 36 acres of glebe.[11] This land he farmed, at first
perhaps because his temperament disliked seeing something not
being put to its proper use, later, as his family grew, because he
needed to. In his poem "To Mr. Wray," he speaks of himself
as "among the furrows striving with hard toil," and we should
remember that this land amounted to almost as much as his
farm at Mapleton.

It is possible also that Dyer chose to live near Rugby (four
miles from Catthorpe) because of friends there, although we do
not now know who they were. In fact, we know of few of Dyer's
Warwickshire and Leicestershire friends. Joseph Harper was the
most important, of course, having presented Dyer to the living
at Catthorpe. Harper's family had been connected with the
manor since the fifteenth century, and though the Caldecotts
had for some time been lords of the manor, Joseph Harper still
retained the advowson of the church. He lived in Chilvers Coton,
just outside Nuneaton, where Dyer probably first met him, and
conducted a mercer's business in Hinckley, Leicestershire.[12]

At Hinckley Dyer seems to have had a circle of friends of
whom today we know the name of only one, Joseph Nutt, an
apothecary and practicing physician there for over fifty years.[13]
He appears in *The Fleece* (I. 440-50) as Nuceus whose pastoral

---

[11] A Glebe Terrier for Catthorpe prepared by Dyer and entirely
in his hand is still preserved at the L.A.O. It was presented at his
first visitation in August, 1742, and states that there were 36 acres
"computed—but mentioned in the Decree of Enclosure to be but
thirty-four" in 7 parcels "lying compact together."

[12] On Harper see Holme, *History of the Midland Counties,* pp.
118-121; John Nichols, *The History and Antiquities of the County
of Leicester* (London, 1810), IV, 601. Dyer himself, in writing to
Duncombe (Duncombe's *Letters,* III, 60), says that Harper gave
him the living of Catthorpe, but the diocesan records (L.A.O., Epis.
Reg. 38, p. 413) give Thomas Caldecott, Esq., as the patron.

[13] See Nichols, *History of Leicester,* IV, 747-8 for a short biography of Joseph Nutt. Nichols quotes (IV, 692, n. 2) his obituary
from the *Leicester Journal,* which mentions his friendship with Dyer.

care is much to be admired. At Catthorpe Dyer must have known everyone in the parish, it was so small, and consequently known the village's most famous resident, the Rev. Mr. Staresmore, a retired clergyman from Hillmorton, Warwickshire. His chief eccentricities were a fondness for making purchases and a great fear of having something stolen. He is said to have locked his servants into their rooms at night, so that they could not take anything, and to have tied dogs (of which he had a great many fierce ones) at the foot of each one of his orchard trees when the fruit was ripe to keep the small boys of the neighborhood from pilfering any. He died in December, 1746, having gone out as usual to feed his dogs in the morning. They, being very eager to obtain their food, jumped up on Mr. Staresmore, who was then aged 79, and pushed him into a pond near the house. He struggled in vain to get out and called for assistance. His servants heard him, but they were still locked in their rooms; a neighbor also heard him groaning and climbed up on the yard wall with an intent to save him, but could get no farther for the dogs. Although Mr. Staresmore was interred in Swinford, Dyer conducted the funeral ceremony; his entry in the register at Catthorpe reads: "Mr. Staresmore died December [Dyer forgot to insert the day of the month], aged 79 and buried at Swinford. Received 10s. of his heir as a mortuary on his death." [14] Booths and stalls were set up around his yard for the disposal of all his accumulation of goods after his death, and several thousand people are said to have attended the sale. No doubt John Dyer was one.

With Dyer's friends we should mention also the one enemy we have found, a Mr. Wheeler of Droitwich, Worcestershire, father of Dyer's predecessor as rector of Catthorpe, Edward Wheeler. Dyer had some dispute with the elder Wheeler in 1743 and visited Worcester about it in May. Failing to arrive

---

[14] Printed in Holme, *History of the Midland Counties,* p. 137. On Staresmore see *Ibid.,* pp. 122-3; Nichols, *History of Leicester,* IV, 76; Samuel Ireland, *Picturesque Views on the Upper, or Warwickshire, Avon* (London, 1795), pp. 30-32. Ireland says Staresmore died Jan. 1, 1746 (o.s.).

at an agreement, he sought the aid of Dr. Mackenzie. The doctor was able to be much more "hard-boiled" than Dyer apparently, for he brought Wheeler around to Dyer's terms on all counts.[15] Just what the difficulty was about is not clear; it may have been over matters connected with Catthorpe church, but a more likely suggestion seems to me to be that it arose out of the settling of the estate of Dyer's aunt, Frances Cocks Ivy Williams. She and Elizabeth Cocks were living together in Monmouth in 1739, Longstaffe said;[16] Frances Williams died in 1740.[17] Her death at this point could both explain Dyer's quarrel and provide a probable date for her sister's coming to live with Dyer's family.

Dyer did not neglect his poetry while in Catthorpe; we hear of *The Fleece* again soon after he settled there, when Edwards wrote to Wray:

I am very glad to hear our friend Dyer has not forgot his Golden Fleece, and shall be very glad if I can contribute one lock of wool towards it: I will try what traditions I can pick up of the first settlement of the manufacture which I think was in this country.[18]

By 1748 Dyer was beyond the purely collecting and was at the writing stage, and was sending sections of his manuscript to his brother Bennet to read. But, as he tells Bennet in sending him

---

[15] See Mackenzie's letter to Dyer, May 25, 1743; *The Patrician*, V (1748), 79. Several draft letters apparently connected with this controversy appear in notebook F. In ink is Dyer's appeal to Dr. Mackenzie to mediate; the others are in much rubbed, often illegible, pencil. One of these concerns a barn and pigsty which were torn down or repaired without somebody's permission apparently. Perhaps this is the source of the trouble.

[16] W. H. D. Longstaffe, *Some Notice of the Fore-elders . . . of the Rev. John Dyer*.

[17] She was buried in Bromyard on May 22, 1740 (Bromyard Parish Register).

[18] Edwards to Wray, Sept. 24, 1742. Ms. Bodl. 1009, p. 255. Edwards was writing from Pudhill, Gloucestershire, where he was visiting his friend Richard Owen Cambridge.

the second installment, he had been ill with what his friends had thought was an ulcerated lung.[19] Clearly his consumptive disorder bothered him before he ever got to Lincolnshire, and cannot be blamed entirely on the fens. And economically he seems to have been in difficult circumstances; in his poem "To Mr. Wray" he wrote that, had it not been for Wray, he,

> Among the furrows striving with hard toil,
> Could seldom have acquired a vacant hour
> To brighten up his thoughts, and sing the Fleece.[20]

What had become of the money he had invested in South Sea stock? What had happened to the money he was lending so affluently in 1735-6? We never learn, but the only conclusion seems to be that some of Dyer's friends were not good risks and failed their obligation to him, thus so reducing his income that he had to work his glebeland and neglect *The Fleece* in order to support his family. So matters stood until 1750 anyway.

Dyer's other literary activity at Catthorpe was concerned mostly with earlier and often completed works. In 1744 two of his poems appeared in John Wesley's *Collection of Moral and Sacred Poems.*[21] *Grongar Hill* had its first reprinting since 1726, and Dyer's verses "Written at Ocriculum" were printed for the first time. How Wesley got the latter is one of the many mysteries of Dyer's life. If the two men had been associating only when they were both contributing to David Lewis' *Miscellany* in 1725-6, we would expect Wesley to have had the 1725 version of the poem, but he prints the 1730 revision. Perhaps they were in touch with one another in the 1740's again.

Grongar Hill was reprinted again, this time with *The Ruins of Rome,* in Dodsley's *Miscellany* in 1748.[22] And in 1750 Dyer sent some verses to Edwards in honor of the publication of *The*

---

[19] *The Patrician,* V (1848), 81.

[20] Willmott, p. xvii.

[21] John Wesley (ed.), *A Collection of Moral and Sacred Poems,* 3 vols. (Bristol, 1744), II, 170-5, 191-3.

[22] Robert Dodsley (ed.), *A Collection of Poems by Several Hands,* 3 vols. (London, 1748), I, 72-100.

Canons of Criticism, Edwards' clever satire on Bishop Warburton. Unfortunately Dyer's poem has been lost, but Edwards' copy of his letter acknowledging it is still in his letter book.[23]

Dyer also turned back, in 1749, to "The Commercial Map." As he explains in his introductory paragraph,[24] a person who was probably Joseph Harper suggested that the "Discourse" on the uses of a commercial map, unaccompanied by the map itself, might be acceptable to the public. Dyer therefore wrote up at least 25 pages of the Discourse—the quantity now preserved in the manuscript in Durham Cathedral which breaks off in the middle of a sentence.[25] Once again the work failed to appear, however. Perhaps Dyer never completed the Discourse; perhaps no publisher could be interested; we have no idea what caused the failure this time.

Dyer's other prose for this period is missing; not only are his sermons lost, but most of his correspondence, an equally lamentable loss, has disappeared. All his letters to Edwards, all but a draft of one letter to Bennet of his letters to his family, all but a few drafts to Mackenzie, and everything to Wray, are gone. And Dyer doubtless had correspondents now unknown to us; Longstaffe published a draft letter to an anonymous lady which is quite modern in its complaint over the difficulty of securing servants.[26] Four letters to Dyer have come down to us, one from Edwards, one from Mackenzie,[27] and two from Benjamin Victor, with whom he seems to have been in touch again in 1742-3.[28] Victor's letters show quite clearly, however, how completely Dyer had lost contact with his friends of the Aaron Hill group.

What we have been saying describes Dyer's life at Catthorpe from 1742 to 1750; it was, as Longstaffe says, uneventful.[29] But

---

[23] Edwards to Dyer, Dec. 20, 1750. Ms. Bodl. 1011, pp. 201-2.

[24] *The Patrician,* V (1848), 81.

[25] The ms. is in bad condition, and consequently some of it may have been lost.

[26] *The Patrician,* V (1848), 81.

[27] *The Patrician,* V (1848), 79.

[28] Victor, *Original Letters,* I, 66-71.

[29] *The Patrician,* V (1848), 81.

in 1750 its tempo increased. During the summer Dyer took a trip to London and South Wales; it seems likely that he had visited both places before since coming to Catthorpe, but this was an unusually important trip. He came to London armed with the manuscript of the first book of *The Fleece,* and was introduced by Wray to Philip Yorke, eldest son of the Earl of Hardwicke, and his wife, the Marchioness Grey. The Yorkes were so favorably impressed with both the poem and Dyer himself that they at once became his patrons. They appointed him Lady Grey's chaplain, a post more honorary than remunerative, no doubt, but symbolic of the sincere attachment they seemed to have for him and of their intention to do more for him. On July 30 Wray wrote to Yorke:

Your postscript is extremely kind, you are too good to remember me and all my friends, but Dyer, I trust, will not discredit the protection you grant him. However awkward he may appear in this bad world, he has two of the characters which qualify for a place in Elysium, *Sacerdos Castus* and *Pius Vates.*[30]

From London Dyer continued on to South Wales, stopping at the Vale of Neath to paint one of the finest of his landscapes (assuming that it was painted on the spot and not from memory). It is signed and dated 1750, and what little we know of its history suggests that Dyer sold it at the time as a means of increasing his slender stipend at Catthorpe.[31] On his return journey he stopped somewhere to take part in a procession to Bishop Blaise—apparently field work for the second book of *The Fleece,* where Bishop Blaise, the patron saint of woolcombers, appears,[32] for Wray reported to Yorke on September 1:

---

[30] Add. Ms. 35,401, fol. 132d.

[31] It was purchased in 1890 by Charles Henry Dyer, a descendant of the poet's brother Thomas, and is owned today by his granddaughter. He bought it from a lady in Surrey whose late husband had secured it from the Marquis of Hastings. It seems, in other words, not to have been in the family before 1890.

[32] *The Fleece,* II. 524-57.

"VALE OF NEATH"

Painted by Dyer in 1750. This landscape has much more color than the (I think) earlier one already reproduced; greens and blues are much in evidence. The original now belongs to a descendant of Dyer's brother Thomas, Miss Lillie Jackson of Truro, to whom I am indebted for permission to reproduce it here.

Dyer has stowed his Argonauts very commodiously in a single bottom, and is now attending on Bishop Blaise in a procession; he is in spirits, but sighs after books, or the neighborhood of them, to consult as he goes on.[33]

Further encouragement was not slow in arriving; in January, 1750/1, Dyer was given the living of Belchford in Lincolnshire, thus increasing his income by £75. The living was a royal presentation, and so in the care of the Lord Chancellor, then Lord Hardwicke, Yorke's father. Dyer was instituted to his new parish on March 26, 1751,[34] and may have intended to keep Catthorpe with it, but before any dispensation or other arrangements could be made, Yorke secured for Dyer the parish of Coningsby in Lincolnshire as well. This parish, the gift of Sir John Heathcote of Normanton in the county of Rutland, Bart. (the father-in-law of one of Yorke's sisters), was accustomed to poets, having had Laurence Eusden as rector at one time.[35] Its stipend was also the best of the three parishes, being £120 per annum, and so Dyer decided to keep his two Lincolnshire parishes and resign Catthorpe at this time.

Yorke and Wray also decided to take advantage of Lord Hardwicke's being High Steward of the University of Cambridge to begin efforts to secure Dyer a degree. Dyer went up to London to help with the circulating of his petition among the Heads of Houses during the vacation.[36] This, of course, explains why Dyer was excused from the episcopal visitation at Leicester on August 1 (and the one at Horncastle, Lincolnshire on August 9, which he was expected to attend as rector of Belchford[37]). On August 2 he left London for Cambridge, where he was detained only two days. He returned to London a Bachelor of Laws, se-

---

[33] Add. Ms. 35,401, fol. 134.

[34] L.A.O., Episcopal Register 38, p. 501.

[35] See DNB under Eusden.

[36] For a more detailed account of the negotiations involved in securing Dyer's degree, see my article, "John Dyer's Degree from Cambridge," *MLN*, LXI (1946), 172-5.

[37] L.A.O., *Liber Cleri*, 20 A, fol. 17 and 20 C, fol. 43.

cured his dispensation to hold his two livings, and then went to
Normanton for the formal presentation of Coningsby. From
there he proceeded to his bishop, presumably at Buckden or
Lincoln, for the official institution, which took place on August
13.[38] And finally, weary but happy, as we can imagine, Dyer
returned to Catthorpe to begin preparing his family to move to
Coningsby.

---

[38] L.A.O., Episcopal Register 38, p. 503. The other details of
Dyer's peregrinations in search of a degree are from Wray's letters
to Yorke of August 6 and 15, 1751; Add. Ms. 35,401, foll. 148d, 150.

CHAPTER VIII

"The Levels of Green Lincoln"

On September 26, 1751, Daniel Wray wrote to Philip Yorke:

Dyer has transported his wife and children and all to Coningsby; he is full of spirits and gratitude to his benefactors, and forgets not his *Fleece*.[1]

And it is *The Fleece* that sets the focus for the remaining years of Dyer's life at Coningsby. His friends were prompt to remind him of his obligations to the Yorkes to finish his poem;[2] he himself wrote to Dr. Mackenzie in 1755 that he considered *The Fleece* a part of his business;[3] and he went about continually with two parchment notebooks in his pockets, one for his sermons and one for notes for *The Fleece*.[4] *The Fleece* dominated or in some way affected almost every one of his activities during his years in Lincolnshire.

Lincolnshire itself proved not unpleasing to him when he first arrived and was still "full of spirits"; shortly after his arrival he wrote a poem on Lincoln Heath in which he expressed his enjoyment of his new surroundings:

---

[1] Add. Ms. 35,401, fol. 151d.

[2] Edwards, for example, wrote to Dyer on Jan. 21, 1752 n.s. regarding *The Fleece*, "the first book of which engaged your noble patrons in your favor, and prompted them to give you this encouragement to proceed in it; let me therefore conjure you not to disappoint their expectations, but to apply yourself with all diligence . . ." (Ms. Bodl. 1011, pp. 325-6).

[3] Dyer to Mackenzie, Jan. 28, 1755; *The Patrician*, V (1848), 221.

[4] *The Patrician*, V (1848), 221.

Nigh are the rising spires of Lamplugh's fane,
Stateliest of Gothic fabrics; and the crags
Of ruins glimmer; every zephyr brings
Into my ears the slow deep-swelling toll
Of the great curfew. So, the traveller,
On Lindum's heath, secure, may bate his pace,
Pleased with the mild descent of purple night.[5]

But unfortunately the fens, damp weather, and ill health soon changed his mind; on December 20, 1751, he wrote some verses beginning:

At length 'mong reeds and mud my bark sticks fast;
So Fate thinks proper, who can now sustain
My tribe with delicacies, frogs and eels,
'Mong reeds and mud; begirt with dead brown lakes,
Whose, perhaps pleasant, shores lie far unseen:
Nor will their habitants the decent face
Of civil man or woman deign approach:
Ev'n Rumour comes not here! . . . [6]

And this remained his attitude for the rest of his life.

When Dyer arrived in Coningsby he found a rectory and garden which had been unoccupied since 1745 and were consequently in a bad state of repair. He at once set to improving the garden and altering the house with his usual energy. His major change was in his own study, where he closed up one window and opened another which gave him a good view of Tattershal Church and Castle, about a mile away. He also put in new paneling in the room—paneling which may still be seen.[7]

Dyer's church work was much heavier than at Catthorpe, but he had assistance. At Belchford the work was taken care of entirely by curates, first by a Mr. Fowler, and from 1753 until Dyer resigned in 1755, by William Pennington, Jr., the son of

---

[5] "A Night Prospect. Written on Lincoln Heath, 1751," lines 1-7; Willmott, p. 113.

[6] *The Patrician*, V (1848), 219-20; a slightly different version appears in Willmott, p. xviii.

[7] Willmott, p. xviii.

one of Dyer's friends, the Rev. William Pennington of Asterby. At Coningsby too Dyer had help. William Gibson, the curate from 1745 to 1751, stayed on and filled in, especially when Dyer was ill.[8] Even so the work was heavy; Dyer was making more entries in the register at Coningsby in a year than he had all nine and a half years at Catthorpe put together. But by this time he had become used to the routine of pastoral work and preparing sermons—including a visitation sermon which he possibly delivered at Horncastle on July 9, 1755.[9] And he was no longer having to farm his glebe land.

In January, 1752, his friends apparently felt that his attention was beginning to wander away from *The Fleece*. Edwards wrote to him:

Mr. Wray tells me you seem to have some other work upon the anvil, but I bar all other engagements till you have acquitted yourself of this [*The Fleece*], which, if it is completed with the same spirit it began with, will bring you great honor and some profit, as well as it will be a proper return for the kindnesses which you have received. You will pardon my earnestness on this occasion, but as I think it is an affair in which your honor is very much interested, and therefore as your friend I am not unconcerned in it, I could not help speaking my mind to you freely as to a friend on this head.[10]

Wray also wrote Dyer at this time, and Dyer took offense at their implied criticism of him.[11] What his other project was is not

---

[8] Gibson was Dyer's curate at Kirkby on Bain in 1756, and the registers at Coningsby for 1756 and 1757 are entirely in his hand. Even earlier he occasionally filled out the printed forms which had become the legal form for recording marriages in 1754, so that it seems probable that he was available to help most of the time. Dyer kept his three-column system of entries in the register even after the printed forms for marriages were introduced, thus recording each marriage twice.

[9] L.A.O., *Liber Cleri* 21 A, fol. 40.

[10] Edwards to Dyer, Jan. 21, 1752 n.s. Ms. Bodl. 1011, p. 326.

[11] Edwards, in his letter to Wray of Feb. 14, 1752, mentions Dyer's "new and revived whims" and Wray's letter to Dyer; on

clear; it may have been only Dyer's building, but Edwards' comments in his letters to Wray suggest that it was a revived "Commercial Map" or some similar project. Dyer, in characteristic fashion, became interested in the chief problems of his parishioners, the drainage of the fens, and formed a library of books on the subject; perhaps he was planning some work on that topic. Or his project may have been antiquarian; at some time while he was at Coningsby he discovered two old Roman encampments in the grounds of Tattershal Park and communicated an account of them to the Antiquarian Society through Wray, who had been elected a Fellow in 1741.[12]

Whatever the rival project was, it did not slow Dyer up too much, for in August he was finishing up the fourth book,[13] and the following January went up to London with the completed poem for his first consultation with his "board of critics." Just as they had supplied Isaac Hawkins Browne as a literary consultant for *The Ruins of Rome,* so now Edwards and Wray brought in outside help to confer with and advise Dyer, in the persons of Dr. Mark Akenside and Richard Roderick. Akenside and Edwards had been drawn together by the attacks upon them of Bishop Warburton, and in 1751 Akenside had written an Ode to Edwards. Roderick had matriculated at Queens' College, Cambridge, in 1728, and there probably knew Wray. He

---

March 23 Edwards wrote, rather defensively, to Wray: "You guess rightly about our friend Dyer; our joint attack does seem to have born too hard upon him, for he calls it a censure; how heavy your pen was I cannot tell, but what I wrote was only an earnest exhortation that he would not engage in any new projects till he has finished his Fleece. However, he tells me he goes on, though but slowly, and that he will send up to you what he has written if he can get franks." (Mss. Bodl. 1011, p. 334; 1012, pp. 7-8).

[12] His account was later included as one of the additions in Richard Gough's edition of Camden's *Britannia,* 2nd ed. (London, 1806), II, 379.

[13] On August 27 Wray reported to Yorke: "Dyer has sent us more than 600 verses of his fourth book; they contain the trading voyage to China, and the route back again through Russia." (Add. Ms. 35,401, fol. 163d).

had later contributed verses to Dodsley's *Miscellany* and aided Edwards with *The Canons of Criticism*. And through Akenside, Joseph Warton also read *The Fleece* in manuscript.[14] Of all these critics, however, Akenside was the most important, and the only one to be mentioned in the surviving letters of Dyer himself.

Edwards and Wray chose badly in selecting Akenside if they thought he would speed up the publication of *The Fleece,* for he was an inveterate reviser and rewriter. He apparently proposed altering the entire plan of the poem at once, for on February 2, 1753, Edwards wrote to Wray

How many books is our friend's Georgic to make? I thought the whole was to have been comprised in four, yet after that you talk of *the other books.* He complained some time ago that his Muse grew stiff; will you not overwork her?[15]

The appearance of Dyer himself at Turrick two months later temporarily quieted Edwards' doubts, but ultimately he was justified, and nothing came of Akenside's fine plans except a lot of wasted effort and further delay.[16]

On these trips to London Dyer usually had some business not connected with *The Fleece* to transact, and occasionally we learn of some of it. From his will we discover that on this trip in 1753, on March 8 he invested one hundred pounds in three

---

[14] Joseph Warton, *An Essay on the Genius and Writings of Pope,* 5th ed. (London, 1806), I, 35n.

[15] Ms. Bodl. 1012, p. 65.

[16] In writing of Dyer's visit, Edwards wrote to Wray on April 4: "He showed me that part of his work which he carried down with him; there was indeed great room for criticism, but he acknowledged the faults with great cheerfulness and said he designed to put it wholly into a new form according to Mr. Roderick's and Dr. Akenside's advice." But a week later, reporting the same visit to Yorke, Edwards said, "The sun must draw up the fogs a little more before his Muse can sum her pens to take a flight, indeed, I wish they are not a little damaged by the damp air of the fen." (Ms. Bodl. 1012, pp. 89, 92).

per cent annuities bought for him from Mr. William Catsford by Collon Lambert and Co.

Dyer was probably on his way home when he stopped to see Edwards. Whether he made any other visits on his way we cannot now say, but in any case he was probably back in Coningsby in time to participate in one of the ceremonies that must have interested him especially during his incumbency there —the marriage on June 25 of Deborah Griffits of Coningsby to Thomas Bass of Hinckley. We can imagine with what eagerness Dyer must have questioned this visitor about his friends in Leicestershire.

The winter of 1753-4 was the worst that Dyer had yet had in Lincolnshire. As he himself reported to Dr. Mackenzie, it had been very hard on him and had even confined him to his bed.[17] For this reason perhaps Dyer did not come up to London for his second consultation with his critics until the summer of 1754. On July 11 Wray wrote to Philip Yorke, now Lord Royston:

> After performing my dinner-duty at the Mitre . . . I retired home to write this letter; when the first thing I met was Dyer just arrived from Lincolnshire; who, I hope, will be some excuse for the futility of it: in order to write this much I must defer examining him till the post comes by; but in general he comes up to be criticized, and to take instructions for finishing the *Fleece*.[18]

Unfortunately Wray continued to write "in general" about Dyer's work, and so did Edwards, so that we learn little of what the Gentle Shepherd actually accomplished during his visit. We hear no more, however, of new plans for the poem.

During the winter of 1754-5 Dyer was weak but better than during the previous winter.[19] It was at this time, Longstaffe be-

---

[17] Dyer to Mackenzie, Jan. 28, 1755; *The Patrician*, V (1848), 221.

[18] Add. Ms. 35,401, fol. 185d.

[19] Dyer to Mackenzie, Jan. 28, 1755; *The Patrician*, V (1848), 221.

PORTRAIT OF HIS DAUGHTER SARAH

Judging by the age of the little girl (b. 1744), I am inclined to assign this painting to Dyer's Coningsby years, perhaps 1752-53. The original is in the possession of Ronald Hylton Smith, Esq.

lieved, that a regular correspondence began between Dyer and Dr. Mackenzie, but it seems more likely that Dyer began at this time the letter book which came to Longstaffe, and that the earlier parts of the correspondence had disappeared even before Longstaffe acquired the papers. He begins his tantalizingly brief excerpts from the correspondence[20] with Mackenzie's letter of December 26, 1754, which refers to an earlier letter of Dyer's, and it seems only natural that these good friends should have communicated regularly before this. Dyer probably turned to letter writing when ill health and the isolation of Lincolnshire separated him from his friends. The few samples which survive indicate that he was an attractive letter writer, and he seems to have had a reputation as such even in his own times, for Edmund Pyle refers to him not as a poet but as "my brother letter-writer John Dyer." [21] It is sad so few of his letters have been preserved.

Dyer's friends Edwards and Wray may have worried about his ever producing *The Fleece,* but his patrons apparently did not. They expressed their confidence in him in very concrete terms in 1755 by giving him the living of Kirkby on Bain with Tumby in exchange for Belchford, an exchange which meant ultimately thirty-five pounds a year more in income. Temporarily, however, Dyer considered himself the loser by the exchange because of the expenses of the seal, dispensation, journeys, and the care of another dilapidated rectory.[22] But this new parish adjoined Coningsby, so that it was very convenient, and Dyer was in much closer touch with it than he ever had been

---

[20] *The Patrician,* V (1848), 220-225.

[21] Albert Hartshorne, *Memoirs of a Royal Chaplain,* 1729-1763 (London, 1905), p. 334. Pyle, writing in 1760 to his old college master, Dr. Samuel Kerrich, about Tory methods of getting into positions of influence, said, "This game is playing now—what the luck will be time will show—as my brother letter-writer John Dyer used to say." I am indebted to Dr. Parker for this reference.

[22] Dyer to Duncombe, Nov. 24, 1756; Duncombe's *Letters,* III, 60. Mackenzie to Dyer, July 15, 1755; *The Patrician,* V (1848), 221.

with Belchford. Although the work was carried on by curates,[23] Dyer performed some of his duties; in 1756 he made out the duplicate register which was sent up to Lincoln, and until late in 1757 he occasionally performed marriages and filled out the printed forms used for recording them.

Dyer's visit to London in the summer of 1755 was the shortest yet of his consultations. On July 9 he attended an episcopal visitation at Horncastle, and sometime between then and August 12, when he appeared before his bishop at Buckden or Lincoln to be instituted to his new parish,[24] he made his trip to London. The fourth and final book of *The Fleece* was apparently the subject of consultation this time, for on July 26 Wray wrote to Lord Royston:

Lord Chancellor's new favor has completed the happiness of Lady Grey's Chaplain; the living of Kirkby was the *angulus* that *denormated* his parish, now it is perfect and *arrondi*. The best evidence of his easy state of mind is the fourth and last book of the *Fleece*, which he has brought up to his board of critics. The topic is the distributing his draperies over all the world; the basis of this must be geographical description, wherein the ideas he has collected as a painter are of singular use. He indeed displays them with great dexterity, and in general we perceive both a flow and a correctness not so common in his later performances. Nor does this book want amendment but in the minuter parts. He tells us likewise he has attended to our objections in the other books, and we now at last make no doubt of having the whole poem before us soon, in order for the press. Akinside and Roderick are assiduous in their good offices, and are fonder of the work and the author than ever.[25]

Dyer probably secured his dispensation to hold his two livings while he was in London,[26] making his institution a stop on his

---

[23] William Gibson was curate, 1755-6, and when he was needed at Coningsby in 1757, a Thomas Neal became curate.

[24] L.A.O., Episcopal Register 38, p. 537.

[25] Add. Ms. 35,401, fol. 196.

[26] It was announced in the *GM* for July (XXV, 334), which appeared, of course, at the end of the month.

homeward journey and arriving in time to be inducted into his new living on August 16.[27] He worked fairly diligently at the long poem before him, but thoughts of his new freedom were too much for him apparently, and even before he had sent off the final manuscript of *The Fleece* he had sent Dr. Mackenzie the seven-line bit of verse beginning "All, all is vanity," and plans for a new and large project. On November 3 Mackenzie acknowledged the verses and said mildly, "You must give your health time to recruit, before you enter upon anything new." [28] But on December 17, after rejoicing with Dyer that *The Fleece* was finally sent off, he spoke more firmly:

it is the nature of our composition that the labour of the mind impairs the health of the body; and therefore I insist upon it, that you shall not consider husbandry in a political light, nor indeed anything else that requires intense thinking, until your strength and spirits are quite restored and sound. I shall not fail to give you any light that may be necessary at a proper time, but not yet.[29]

Perhaps "husbandry in a political light" had been his proposed project in 1752 also.

Unfortunately Dyer's board of critics were still not satisfied, and he had to make one more trip to London for *The Fleece*. Either on the way or after he arrived he slept in a damp bed which, with his constitution weakened by the winter anyway, at once put him to bed ill,[30] and Dr. Akenside had to give

---

[27] The only entry in Dyer's hand in the main register (exclusive of the printed marriage forms) at Kirkby reads: "John Dyer was inducted into this rectory August 16, 1755."

[28] *The Patrician,* V (1848), 222.

[29] *The Patrician,* V (1848), 222-3.

[30] On April 20, 1756 Mackenzie wrote Dyer: "I was grieved to find by yours of the 3d current, that you were laid in a damp bed. If they sin through ignorance or poverty who commit that crime, there may be some excuse for them, but if through laziness or malevolence, they deserve hanging . . . Pray let not your modesty for the future, throw you into such obvious dangers." *The Patrician,* V (1848), 223.

medical as well as literary advice. Akenside fortunately was able to prescribe adequately, and Dyer was apparently able to carry out the main objectives of his trip in spite of the doubts of Thomas Edwards, who wrote on April 28:

I am glad to hear that Dr. Akenside has recovered Dyer again, but has Dyer recovered his poetical vein? Alas, I fear we shall have no *Fleece* at last.[31]

And even after he returned home Dyer was apparently ill, for on a later occasion Dr. Mackenzie warned Dyer to be careful, lest "they will put you into a damp bed, and make you ill for half a year." [32]

He was well enough by the end of the summer, however, to receive a visit from Dr. and Mrs. Mackenzie, planned for in the doctor's letter of August 2 and thanked for in his letter of October 25.[33] On their return to Sutton Coldfield the Mackenzies stopped in Worcester and there saw Dr. and Mrs. Greenwood, who were delighted to hear that *The Fleece* was finished; they had seen only the first book. Apparently Dyer had completed his last pre-publication revision by October; by November 24, when he wrote to Duncombe, he had sent his manuscript up to Dodsley.[34] In this case Edwards and Wray were able to achieve their wish and have Dodsley be the publisher.

Meanwhile Dyer was writing other verse. In his letter of August 2, 1756 Dr. Mackenzie acknowledged Dyer's verses in honor of the doctor's *History of Health* which had just been published. The earthquake which had destroyed Lisbon on November 1, 1755, had made an unusually strong impression on Dyer because he had probably visited there on his way to Italy, in 1724, although it seems to have affected all Englishmen

---

[31] Edwards to Wray; Ms. Bodl. 1012, p. 256, printed in *The Poetical Works of Mark Akenside,* Aldine Edition, ed. Alexander Dyce (London, 1866), p. lxii, note 3.

[32] *The Patrician,* V (1848), 225.

[33] *The Patrician,* V (1848) 223-4.

[34] Duncombe's *Letters,* III, 59.

greatly. Consequently one morning in 1756 he woke with some verses all composed in his mind about the earthquake.

And in September began the correspondence from which the most of his share has survived. William Duncombe, who with his son John was editing a collection of translations and imitations of the works of Horace, wrote asking Dyer to contribute and seeking permission to inscribe to Dyer an imitation of the 26th ode of the first book. Dyer replied, in a letter dated September 27, 1756:

I gratefully acknowledge the favour of yours, which does me an honour; and I am much obliged to your son for his high compliment, the more so as 'tis the compliment of one of fine taste, who has imitated the ode with great delicacy, and I congratulate the public, who is likely to receive a better translation of Horace than the celebrated one of Mr. Francis. I wish I could please my vanity in answering that other compliment, which comes to me in the shape of a request, but really I never attempted any translation, or imitation of Horace, except his 22nd ode in the first book, which was mislaid and lost above 30 years ago.[35]

John Duncombe not only published his tribute to Dyer,[36] but later the better part of Dyer's six letters to his father as well.

All the revising and correcting he had done seems to have gotten into Dyer's blood; even after Dodsley had the poem, he wrote to Duncombe, "I did not think this a fit season for its

---

[35] The letter which Duncombe prints as of Nov. 24, 1756 (*Letters*, III, 56-61) is a composite of at least two, of which I own the complete original of one, that of Sept. 27, 1756, made up of the paragraph here quoted and (deleting the clause "which is just sent up to Mr. Dodsley") the third paragraph printed by Duncombe. The other letter was cut up at an early date; through the courtesy of Mr. W. S. Lewis, I have one strip of it, totaling nine lines, all printed in Duncombe.

[36] Mr. [William] Duncombe, J[ohn] Duncombe, and other hands, *The Works of Horace in English Verse* (London, 1756), I, 101.

publication, but my friend Mr. Wray overcame me." [37] Apparently Wray was beginning to share Edward's fear that "his Muse is too much laden with thick clay." [38] Dyer, however, continued to make corrections in his own copy of *The Fleece* until he died.[39]

The poem was finally published on March 15, 1757.[40] What notice was taken of it was highly favorable,[41] but in general the public was apathetic, and a second edition was never called for, the collected editions of Dyer's works which began to appear in 1761 supplying any demand that might have arisen later.

Dyer looked upon his poem as a georgic, and as such it was regarded and judged by his contemporaries. That meant that, following the lead of Virgil, the poem was primarily didactic, but that its precepts were of universal interest and had a national appeal.[42] Dyer was unusual, among eighteenth-century writers in this tradition, in that his precepts, especially in the first two books, were based on personal observation and experience more than on reading. His years among the sheep raisers of Leicester-

---

[37] Dyer to Duncombe, Jan. 31, 1757; Duncombe's *Letters,* III, 65; see also Dyer to Duncombe, Nov. 24, 1756; Duncombe's *Letters,* III, 59.

[38] Edwards to Wray, July 19, 1755; Ms. Bodl. 1012, p. 220a.

[39] Now in the possession of Dr. Parker. Dyer's presentation copy to Dr. Mackenzie, containing some of the same revisions, was recently (1955) offered for sale by the bookseller Arnold Muirhead, of St. Albans, Herts. in his catalogue "The Lime Tree Miscellany," No. 10. This copy contained a half dozen or so corrections.

[40] See the advertisements in the *London Chronicle,* I (March 1-3, 3-5, 12-15, 1757), 216c, 224b, 256c; *London Evening Post* (March 12-15, 1757) 3b.

[41] See, for example, *The Monthly Review,* XVI (April 1757), 328-340; *London Chronicle,* I (March 22-24), 284-6; *The Critical Review,* III (May 1757), 402-15.

[42] The reviewer in *The Monthly Review* was Dr. James Grainger, himself later the author of a similar georgic entitled *The Sugar-Cane* (on his authorship of this review, see Willmott, pp. xxiv-xxv, and Nichols' *Illustrations,* VII, 226n). On p. 329 Grainger has conveniently listed the main conventions to be observed by poets writing georgics.

shire stood him in good stead. He was also the first to make his appeal to national interest through the "Arts of Trade," thus creating a new minor genre sometimes referred to as the "mercantile epic." And many of his favorite ideas for social welfare were woven into his fabric also, such as the inclosure of common fields (II. 107-33) and his support of workhouses for the poor (III. 234-302).

Even the eighteenth century, however, with all its emphasis on the didactic, did not like unrelieved instruction. As the reviewer of *The Fleece* says in *The Monthly Review*, "The attention ought often to be awakened by pleasing and natural episodes and digressions." It is these episodes and digressions (which are mainly descriptive), if anything, that will take the modern reader back to *The Fleece*. There are a number of them that rise above the prosaic level of much eighteenth-century blank verse (including some of Dyer's own): the passage describing the sheep-shearing festival at the end of book I (601-720), and the descriptions of rivers at the end of book III (557-632). This same change in taste can be observed by the end of the eighteenth century, when *The Fleece* is spoken of as a descriptive rather than as a didactic poem.[43] As Dyer's mercantile theories of economics became obsolescent, and other precepts unnecessary,[44] it was inevitable that the attraction of the poem should shift from its precepts to what were actually more universal and lasting, the descriptive passages and episodes. As Wordsworth said, Dyer was the

> Bard of the Fleece, whose skilful genius made
> That work a living landscape fair and bright.[45]

---

[43] "Memoirs of the Life of the Reverend John Dyer, L.L.B.," *The Universal Magazine*, XCII (April 1793), 241-3; Nathan Drake, *Literary Hours*, Nos. 12 and 13, 1st ed. (Sudbury, 1798); 3rd ed. (London, 1804), I, 209-57.

[44] For example, Dyer advocates the abolition of the slave trade (IV. 189-208); with the emancipation of the slaves in all the British Empire in 1833, British interest in the slave trade decreased.

[45] "To the Poet, John Dyer," in *The Complete Poetical Works of William Wordsworth*, Cambridge Edition (Boston, 1904), p. 540.

The remaining months of Dyer's life are a chronicle of increasingly bad health. As late as the 31st of January he had written to Duncombe about coming to London in the spring,[46] and he may actually have taken a trip with his family to visit the Mackenzies in February.[47] But his final illness set in soon after; on March 19 he wrote Duncombe that he dreaded even the posture of writing,[48] and his letters grow shorter and shorter. In May he was "in mortar" repairing a barn which had blown down and at last doing something about the decayed rectory at Kirkby;[49] how much he had failed is nowhere more clear than in the contrast between his attitude toward this work and the ease with which he had done similar work at Coningsby less than six years earlier.

Even the verse which he wrote during this last year shows the effect of his sickness. On March 3 Dr. Mackenzie acknowledged Dyer's paraphrase from the twelfth chapter of Ecclesiastes, suggesting an emendation and reporting that Miss Clayton had requested copies of it to send to her friends in London.[50] A month later Mackenzie, still awaiting his copy of *The Fleece*, commented upon Dyer's lines to his son.[51] These too were requested by the ever loyal but none too discriminating Miss Clayton. And in October Dyer sent some verses to Joseph

---

[46] Duncombe's *Letters*, III, 62-3.

[47] Mackenzie's letter of Feb. 18 encourages Dyer's plans, and the doctor's letter of March 3 asks Jacky to return a pair of scissors, suggesting that they might have been carried away recently rather than left in Coningsby the preceding autumn. *The Patrician*, V (1848), 224.

[48] Duncombe's *Letters*, III, 66.

[49] Duncombe's *Letters*, III, 70. On April 11 Dr. Mackenzie wrote: "I flattered myself that the cold bath would have made you as hardy as a Laplander, impenetrable to snow or rain; but I find you are still the same puny creature I knew some years ago, at Worcester . . . Pray let not the frankness of your heart induce you to build more at Kirkby than is quite necessary." *The Patrician*, V (1848), 225.

[50] *The Patrician*, V (1848), 224.

[51] *The Patrician*, V (1848), 225.

Harper. Dyer apparently wanted to leave a tribute in verse to each of his best friends. Most of them he had woven into *The Fleece,* or written pieces for on some other occasion, but he had missed Harper. Rather pathetically he writes: "Indeed, I have not paid you off cleverly, as I grow dull through extreme bad health." [52] A week later, on October 13, he made his will.

His consumption finally conquered, and Dyer died in December, 1757, and was buried on the 15th at Coningsby.[53] Although he himself had composed three epitaphs for himself, and his family had prepared one elaborate one,[54] none exists today in the church, and the only memorial to him at Coningsby is the pair of bells which hang in the church tower.[55] Apparently his family thought that the bells were a sufficient memorial, and the more one thinks of them, the more one feels that nothing could be more appropriate for Dyer than a memorial that could be used, especially one that, in summoning people to church, would be helping to further his own work.

By the terms of his will, Dyer left the life use of Dowell's Farm in Higham to his wife, in lieu of a jointure of thirty

---

[52] Willmott, p. xvi.

[53] The tradition is that he was buried in the chancel, and this is probably correct. A correspondent of the Carmarthenshire Antiquarian Society wrote that Dyer was buried in Llangathen church with a stone to his memory placed in the wall near the Llether Cadvan Chapel (see *TCAS,* I [1905-6], 86). Such a legend is supported by an entry in the Llangathen register of the burial of a John Dyer on Jan. 5, 1758. Unfortunately for the legend the Llether Cadvan Chapel has been done over since the correspondent wrote and all traces of any stone removed, and the entry in the register is undoubtedly for a John Dyer, son of William Dyer, baptized four days earlier.

[54] *The Patrician,* V (1848), 227-9. The 3 by himself are in notebook B.

[55] The antiquarian Richard Gough visited Coningsby in Sept. 1782 and could find no stone to Dyer then, so probably none ever existed (*Westminster Magazine,* XI [March, 1783], 128). One bell has been recast; the other bears the inscription "1757 [ornament] The Rev. Jn. Dyer Rector."

pounds agreed to before their marriage; at her death the farm
was to go to his son John, who also received Paget's Farm in
Higham. Lower Nicholson in Hatfield went to his daughter
Elizabeth on condition of her paying her sister Sarah £400
within a year; as there is no mention of Mapleton, or of any
property in Worcestershire, he must have disposed of all the
other land he inherited from the Cocks family. His daughter
Catherine he provided with £400 also: the annuities he had
bought in 1753, and three sums of £100 each, owed to him by
the Rev. William Pennington and his daughter Elizabeth, by
William Burcham of Coningsby, and by Joseph Hammerton of
Horncastle. If he had lost money earlier by lending it to friends,
apparently he had not abandoned the practice. Other items
such as money due him for tythes and back rent, and money in
the hands of Joseph Harper and Daniel Wray, he directed his
wife to collect and divide equally in five parts amongst herself
and her children. Everything else except certain books he left
to his wife. His books on architecture and antiquities went to
his brother Thomas, those on trade and navigation to Joseph
Harper, those on the drainage of fens to the Rev. William
Pennington of Asterby, and a red book of drawings to Daniel
Wray. His manuscripts were left to his brother Thomas in trust
for his son John.[56]

Dyer's family settled at this time in Hinckley, to be near
Mrs. Dyer's brother, John Strong Ensor, who at her death in
1760 became the guardian of the poet's children. The later
history of the family may be followed in detail in Longstaffe's
article in *The Patrician*.[57]

*   *   *   *   *

As we look back over the life of John Dyer, poet, painter,
farmer, parson, the most interesting aspect of it is his search for

---

[56] The will was at Somerset House. It was witnessed by Dyer's
curate William Gibson and his wife Ann Gibson, and William
Simpson. It was proved in March, 1758, administration being
granted to the executrix, Sarah Dyer.

[57] *The Patrician*, V (1848), 232-5.

some reconciliation between his ideals and his everyday actions. We have expressed this as a conflict between the dreamy romantic and the practical man of business in Dyer; fundamentally it is a timeless problem, but as Dyer experienced and solved it, it is typically an eighteenth-century affair. Expressed in purely literary terms, it is essentially the same conflict as the struggle between classical and romantic tendencies which can be exemplified in so many different ways during the century.

One of these ways is the struggle throughout the century between sentimentalism in its various manifestations and its opponents, and it is into this conflict that the story of John Dyer's life fits most perfectly. As a young man, under the influence of such figures as Aaron Hill and Sir Richard Steele, he absorbed the fundamental precepts of sentimentalism before they had become widespread: a conviction of the inadequacy of reason to prove the existence of God and to control man's behavior; a belief that some of the passions can be directed to good ends and that therefore man is perfectible; and finally, the emphasis on pleasing sensations and sentiments, the most pleasing of which is "doing good," or benevolism. This philosophy satisfied him for a while; he dreamed of "doing universal good," of "a wider sphere to move in," of "the flight of an endless ascent." But it appealed to only one side of his nature, the romantic, and so did not completely fill his needs.

The practical side of his nature demanded something more specific. Theologically this need was met by the rationalism of Clarke and Wollaston. It was clear and precise: it proved the existence of God to his satisfaction by reason alone; it was the sole basis for virtuous behavior; it recognized more realistically than did sentimentalism the evil that he saw in the world, without in any sense discouraging his urge to do something about it. And the harmony of the universe, which made the conformity of moral actions to reason possible, appealed to his innate sense of orderliness.

In his private life and everyday activities this need was answered by entering the church and by the entirely new line of thought which had been opened to him by his reading in the field of trade and commerce. He became, after Defoe, one of the first literary figures to see where the future development of England's greatness was to be, and he made it his work to aid in that development, both through his pastoral work and through *The Fleece*. The change in his attitude may be seen by contrasting the Naamanism of his "Epistle to a Friend in Town" with the opening lines of his poem "To Mr. Wray," written late in life:

> I wonder at their turn of mind who seek
> Lone shades and melancholy cells, remote
> From each occasion of performing good,
> While all the busy world around them rolls:
> While vice contends with virtues; and each street
> The preacher's voice invokes. Though the fell wolf
> Pursues the lamb, and the fall'n struggling ox
> Dies in the ditch, they lend no helping hand,
> Yet dream, by contemplation, best to serve
> Omnipotence and Wisdom.

Dyer had turned his back on romantic solitude and melancholy as a philosophy of life.

This change can nowhere be better seen than through a comparison of *Grongar Hill* and *The Fleece*. Joseph Warton admired the "oblique" instruction in the earlier poem,[58] where the main emphasis is on description and the feelings of the poet about the scenes he is describing; moralizing is introduced casually and gracefully when it seems appropriate—when the scene suggests it. In *The Fleece* instruction is the main point of the poem; description is now the secondary matter and purely ornamentation. As a result of this change in emphasis, *The Fleece* seems today less a precursor of the romantic movement than does *Grongar Hill*, although *The Fleece* was published over thirty years later. And because of this fact, the generally roman-

---

[58] Joseph Warton, *Essay on the Genius and Writings of Pope*, 5th ed. (London, 1806), I, 34.

tically inclined criticism of the past two centuries has tended to look upon Dyer's works as, in his own words,

> The unfathomable gulf where Asshur lies
> O'erwhelmed, forgotten; and high-boasting Cham;
> And Elam's haughty pomp; and beauteous Greece;
> And the great queen of earth, imperial Rome.[59]

Much, perhaps, deserves to be forgotten, along with Asshur, Cham, and Elam. But I hope that a reconsideration of Dyer's works in the light of his life and his times will reveal to the twentieth-century reader much more than *Grongar Hill* that can be classed with "beauteous Greece, And the great queen of earth, imperial Rome."

---

[59] *The Ruins of Rome*, 542-5 (concluding 4 lines).

Index

This is primarily an index of names of persons and places. A brief subject index, of topics specifically connected with John Dyer, will be found in a separate alphabetization under his name.